Isabel Willshaw is a lectu
Higher Education.

Companion German Grammar

ISABEL WILLSHAW

Pan Books London and Sydney

Also available

Companion French Grammar
Companion Spanish Grammar

First published 1983 by Pan Books Ltd,
Cavaye Place, London SW10 9PG
9 8 7 6 5 4 3 2 1
ISBN 0 330 30108 X

Photoset by Parker Typesetting Service, Leicester
Printed and bound in Great Britain by
Hazell Watson & Viney Limited,
Member of the BPCC Group,
Aylesbury, Bucks

Contents

Introduction

You may have decided to buy this German grammar because you have been studying German for some time but have never really understood the system behind it. Perhaps you lost track of grammar when you missed a few classes. Perhaps you used a coursebook which didn't give any grammar explanation. Perhaps you already own a German grammar but can't make head nor tail of it.

This book is designed to make German grammar accessible and understandable to people who do not wish a dense reference work. It aims to keep the explanations as clear and simple as possible and to concentrate on those items of grammar essential to everyday conversation. It is also aimed at the person who enjoys getting to grips with the grammar of a foreign language and who may already have learned one or more other foreign languages.

However, the most important idea behind this grammar is this: grammar is your *tool* and *not* your *master.* Grammar is merely the structure, the system of the language. Although it is important, it is not an end in itself. Living people do not talk or read or write grammar. So keep things in perspective. It is far more important to get your message across and make a few grammar mistakes than to keep quiet because you are afraid of making mistakes. People want to hear *what* you have to say. *How* you say it is definitely less important to them. Anyway, don't you occasionally make mistakes in your own language?

I am not trying to pretend that German grammar is easy. Wherever possible I have tried to reduce the complexities and point out the minimum you can get away with knowing. The *Learn by Heart* sections should help you to deal with very common situations without your always having to remember all the rules.

How to use this book

This book is not a course book. It is a reference book which can be used together with a course book. It is small enough to take away on a visit to Germany. Because it is compact and deliberately focuses on certain high-priority areas of grammar, it is not an all-embracing, exhaustive reference work. It does not claim to cover all the subtleties and finer points of German grammar.

The book is arranged according to grammar points. These are listed on the Contents page, and the Index contains references to non-technical terms as well as grammar points. There is a Glossary of grammatical terms on page 167.

It is useful to bear in mind that not all grammar points are equally important. This grammar has been designed primarily for people who want to communicate with confidence in German.

Each grammar point is subdivided and contains information under various headings:
INTRODUCTION. This gives you a general introduction to the grammar point, and often points out what sort of situations you will find it particularly helpful in.
EXPLANATION. This gives you some extra information about the grammar point, helps you to beware of traps and use it correctly.
WHEN TO USE. This tells you in some detail the types of situation where the grammar point is appropriate.
HOW TO USE. This gets down to the 'nitty gritty', the hard-core information about the grammar point.
LEARN BY HEART. This is a very important section because it gives you the chance to practise what you have just learned. Once you have digested the information about the grammar point there are exercises in which you write down a missing part of the German sentence. The English translation is given alongside and the correct answer is at the bottom of the same page. This enables you to check your answer immediately and then you can cover up one side or the other to help you learn by heart. If possible, you are advised to write out the German sentences on a separate piece of paper. All the *Learn by Heart* examples have been carefully chosen because you will either come across them or want to say them yourself when in Germany.

Help yourself

Your attitude to language learning

Many of us have learned or tried to learn a foreign language at school or college. For some it was a wonderful experience, but for many it was a great disillusionment. It is easy to blame others – textbook writers, teachers, poor facilities and so on, but very often the learner's own attitude contributes to the sense of disillusionment too. It takes native speakers a good 15 to 20 years to learn all the subtleties of a language. How can you possibly expect to attain this standard under very different circumstances?

1. Aiming for perfection is unrealistic – so lower your expectations.

2. All foreign language learning is an experiment. In order to improve you *have* to make mistakes because it is only through your mistakes that you will learn.

3. Nobody will think you are stupid if you try. They may very well think that you are stupid or intensely boring if you are always struck dumb for fear of making a mistake.

4. Try to develop a sensitivity to other people speaking the language. If you are not quite sure how to say something, try it out and ask others for help. Listen and digest what they say – this is the best way of refining your own ability in the foreign language.

So don't aim for native-speaker perfection straightaway, but do aim to improve your personal performance at your own pace. This means keeping your eyes and ears open, and asking questions, looking up things which puzzle you. Remind yourself why you are learning German – your motivation is the most important single factor in ensuring your progress.

If your attitude to language learning is positive and realistic, you will go a long way and make a lot of friends. Let your motto be 'I'll have a go.' The Germans say 'Fragen kostet nichts' – it costs nothing to ask. So have a go, have fun with your German grammar – and you'll do it!

About you and German grammar

Help yourself to learn by using what you know already. As a speaker of English, you already have a great deal of useful knowledge which will help you to learn German vocabulary and grammar.

English and German used to be one language, and many of the features of the two present-day languages are still very closely related.

1. VOCABULARY

If you look at words like **Mann** (man), **Freund** (friend), **Sohn** (son), **Tochter** (daughter), **Brot** (bread), **Butter** (butter), **Milch** (milk) etc. you can see how closely many of the simple everyday words are linked. In addition, there are many more sophisticated, Latin-based words which the two languages have in common: **Professor**, **Akademie**, **Museum**, **Universität**, **Revolution**, **Opposition**, **Koalition** etc.

2. GRAMMAR

It will help you to understand German grammar if you reflect that English used to have a grammar system which was very similar to present-day German. English used to have lots of different endings, but we have gradually got rid of most of them. In English, we now use word order instead of endings to show for example whether a noun is the subject or object of a verb.

But we still have some traces of the old system:
We make the plural by adding -s or -es or -en etc. to nouns.
We still use he/him, I/me, who/whom to show subject/object.
We still have verb endings: I sit/he sits/you sit.
We also have lots of strong verbs: sing, sang, sung; write, wrote, written etc.
If you keep this in mind, you will accept perhaps more readily that although German may seem to be a 'difficult' language, it is in fact based on the same system as our own language.

Verbs

INTRODUCTION

Verbs are words like 'do', 'eat', 'drink', 'sit', 'stand'. They are often action words but they can also be words like 'be', 'stay', 'lie', 'wait' etc. which describe a state of affairs with no movement, a position etc. Every sentence, no matter how short, contains a verb. The verb is the hub of the sentence – the rest of the sentence is formed around it. When you look up a German verb in a dictionary, you will find various pieces of information:

1. The form of the verb you see in the dictionary will end in **-en**.

spiel*en* (to play) **mach*en*** (to do) etc.

We call this the *infinitive*, the reference form of the verb, which in English always has 'to' in front of it, and in German always ends in **-en**. If you take away the **-en** ending you are left with the *stem* of the verb, the basis to which you can add various endings.

2. Sometimes the dictionary will say 'v.t.' or 'v.i.' (verb transitive or verb intransitive). Transitive means that the verb can take a direct object or accusative (see p.84 if you do not understand these terms). So words like 'eat', 'drink' etc. are transitive because you can eat or drink *something*. But words like 'go' and 'lie' are intransitive because you can't go or lie something.

EXPLANATION

In order to use a verb, you have to know:

1. what type of verb it is;
2. what person or thing is doing the action;
3. what tense the verb is in;
4. The role of the verb in that particular sentence.

1. Types of verbs

There are several types of verbs in German:

a) weak verbs or regular verbs;
b) strong verbs or irregular verbs (see p.27);
c) separable verbs (see p.28);
d) modal verbs (see p.34);
e) reflexive verbs (see p.39).

2. The person or thing doing the action

This could be:

Singular

ich I
du (informal) you
Sie (formal) you
er he, it
sie she, it
es it
der Mann, das Restaurant or any other singular noun
Susanne or any other person
man ('one' = person not specified)

Plural

wir we
ihr (informal) you
Sie (formal) you
sie they
die Männer, die Bücher or any other plural noun
Susanne und Manfred or any other people

Sometimes grammar books refer to the 1st, 2nd and 3rd person.

1st person	=	I, we
2nd person	=	you
3rd person	=	he, she it, one, they + all nouns and names of people, places etc.

3. Tenses

Tenses are the forms of the verb which tell us when the action is/will be/was/taking place. The most important tenses are: present; imperfect (= continuous past); perfect (= past); pluperfect (= past, one step further back than perfect); future. Each tense is formed differently. Some are variations of the stem + endings. Others are formed by combining the main verb with a second verb. We will also look at other forms, such as commands, the subjunctive etc.

4. Role of the verb

In a simple sentence you will find the verb in the second position if the sentence is a statement (see p.51). However, in more complicated sentences where there are two or more verbs, the rules are different. See: modal verbs (p.34); conjunctions (p.73); and sentence structure (p.56).

Present tense

INTRODUCTION

In English we can say either, 'I read the newspaper' (implying habitual action), or 'I am reading the newspaper' (at this moment). These are both present tense forms but have different meanings. In German, this difference does not exist. There is only one present tense to cover both meanings. So for both of the above statements you would say, **'Ich lese die Zeitung'**. This is one of the relatively few examples of German being simpler than English!

WHEN TO USE

You use the present tense in German:

a) To talk about what habitually happens.
   Ich lese jeden Morgen die Zeitung. I read the newspaper every morning.

b) To talk about what is happening now.
   Ich lese gerade die Zeitung. I'm reading the newspaper just now.

c) To talk about what is going to happen in the near future.
   Ich komme nächste Woche nach Hause. I'm coming home next week.

HOW TO USE

1. Weak Verbs (= regular or normal verbs)

Take **-en** off the infinitive and add these endings to the stem:

Singular		*Plural*	
ich	**-e**	**wir**	**-en**
du	**-st**	**ihr**	**-t**
Sie	**-en**	**Sie**	
er, sie, es		**sie**	**-en**
man		plural noun	
noun	**-t**	plural name	
name			

N.B. For details about the use of **du/ihr** see p.103.

Take the verb **spielen** (to play). You say:

ich spiel*e*		**wir spiel*en***	
du spiel*st*		**ihr spiel*t***	
Sie spiel*en*		**Sie spiel*en***	
er, sie, es **man** **der Mann** **Manfred**	**spiel*t***	**sie** **die Frauen** **Anna und Maria**	**spiel*en***

If the stem ends in **-t** or **-d**, e.g. **baden** (to bathe) or **arbeiten** (to work), you will have to add an extra **e** to the **er/sie/es** form in order to be able to say it. Otherwise you will sound as if you have a terrible stammer!

Er bad*et* **Sie arbeit*et***

2. Strong verbs (= irregular verbs)

Take **-en** off the infinitive and add the same endings to the stem as for weak verbs. *But* sometimes there will be a change in the stem for the **du** and **er/sie/es** forms. How can you tell whether there is a change? In a dictionary you might see: **fahren** (¨), or you will find the **du** (2nd person singular) and the **er/sie/es** (3rd person singular) forms written out for you: **du fährst, er fährt.**

The change is usually quite a radical change in vowel sound.

infinitive	*present tense stem changes*	
schlafen	**du schläfst**	**er schläft**
lesen	**du liest**	**er liest**
essen	**du ißt**	**er ißt**

Now check with your list of strong verbs (p.163) and write out the **du** and **er/sie/es** forms of the following very common verbs: **nehmen, sprechen, sehen, helfen, tragen, treffen, werfen, geben.** When you have written them down, practise saying them aloud. Make sure you pronounce the Umlaut (¨) clearly if there is one, as well as the difference between **e, i,** and **ie, ei.** Write down the English meaning of the verb at the same time.

3. Present tense summary

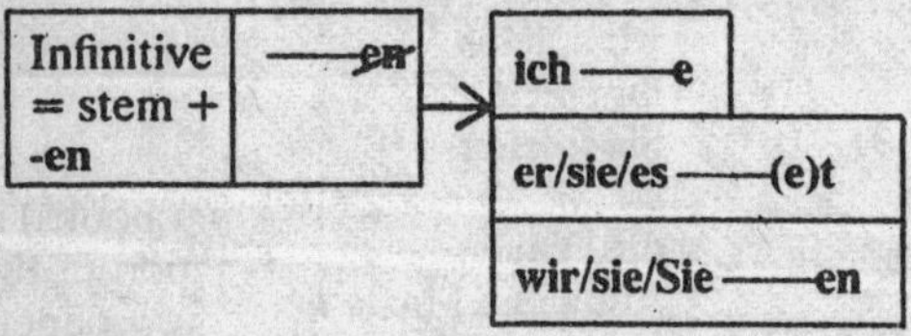

N.B.
strong verbs –
stem change?
er/sie/es —?— (e)t

4. Sein

The only verb which doesn't fit into the scheme of things is **sein** (to be) (see p.165). The present tense is:

ich bin	**wir sind**
du bist	**ihr seid**
er/sie/es ist	**sie/Sie sind**

PRACTICE/LEARN BY HEART

Talking about your daily routine. Fill in the blanks with the correct form of the verb. They are all in the present tense.

1. **Wir .... um acht Uhr.** — We have breakfast at 8 o'clock.
2. **Ich .... die Kinder um Viertel vor neun zur Schule.** — At a quarter to nine I drive the children to school.
3. **Dann .... ich die Zeitung.** — Then I read the newspaper.
4. **Dann .... ich zur Arbeit.** — Then I go to work.
5. **Abends .... wir Musik.** — In the evenings we listen to music.
6. **Wir .... Freunde.** — We visit friends.

ANSWERS

1. frühstücken. 2. fahre. 3. lese. 4. gehe. 5. hören. 6. besuchen.

Imperfect tense

INTRODUCTION

The imperfect tense (called Präteritum in German grammar books) is used for description, for narrative and for continuous action in the past. You are most likely to come across it when reading newspapers and stories.

WHEN TO USE

In practice you will often find yourself using the imperfect tense of:

sein (to be)	**ich/er/sie/es war** (was)	**wir/Sie/sie waren** (were)
haben (to have)	**ich/er/sie/es hatte** (had)	**wir/Sie/sie hatten** (had)

because that's how you say where you have been, what was wrong with you, whether you enjoyed yourself etc. You will hear and read other verbs in the imperfect tense, but they are quite easy to guess. By all means spend some time learning these, but you may find it more profitable to concentrate on other, higher priority areas of German grammar. As long as you can use **sein** and **haben** and can make intelligent guesses at the other verbs, you will get along very well.

HOW TO USE

1. Weak verbs

Take off the **-en** ending from the infinitive, add **-te** for the singular and **-ten** for the plural and **Sie** forms:

sagen (to say)

ich sag*te*	**wir sag*ten***
er/sie/es/sag*te*	**sie sag*ten***
	Sie sag*ten*

Put another way:

Infinitive —~~en~~ → ich/er/sie/es —te

wir/sie/Sie —ten

2. Strong verbs

A full list of strong verbs appears on pages 163–164. Take off the **-en** ending of the infinitive. There is always a significant change of stem. There is no ending for the singular, but in the plural **-en** is added to the changed stem.

schlafen (to sleep)
ich/er/sie/es schlief **wir/sie/Sie schliefen**

fahren (to travel)
ich/er/sie/es fuhr **wir/sie/Sie fuhren**

Put another way:

Infinitive ~~en~~	→	change of stem	→	**ich/er/sie/es** no ending **wir/sie/Sie** add **-en**

PRACTICE

Now do the same for: **sehen, lesen, essen, ziehen, trinken, finden, geben.** (Answers at foot of page.)

Perfect tense

INTRODUCTION

'Perfect' is another word for 'completed'. You use the perfect tense in German when you talk about completed action in the past. We do this in two ways in English:

1. Simple past tense: I *ate* an apple.
   He *waved* goodbye.
2. Past tense with 'have' + ——ed or ——en:
   I *have fixed* the doorhandle.
   He'*s mended* the fuse.
   Have you *eaten* your breakfast?

ANSWERS

sah/sahen, las/lasen, aß/aßen, zog/zogen, trank/tranken, fand/fanden, gab/gaben.

The examples under 2. are much closer to the present time, but in both 1. and 2. the action is complete.

You use the perfect for both of these in German, and you will need to use it whenever you are talking about the past.

HOW TO USE

To form the perfect tense, you use the present tense of **haben (ich habe, er hat, Sie haben** etc.) + the *past participle* of your verb. The past participle is the '—ed' or '—en' form you find in English '(have) mend*ed*', 'eat*en*' etc.

To make a past participle in German:
Take the **-en** ending off the infinitive.
Add **ge-** to the beginning of most verbs.
Add **-t** or **-et** ending to weak verbs. (This is parallel to adding '-ed' to English regular verbs.) Add **-en** ending to strong verbs (parallel to '-en' in English irregular verbs).

The past participle for strong verbs often has a radical change of stem, so check with the verb list on p.163 until you have learned them. Very often you can guess them because they are similar to the English forms:

singen	**gesungen**	sing	sung
trinken	**getrunken**	drink	drunk

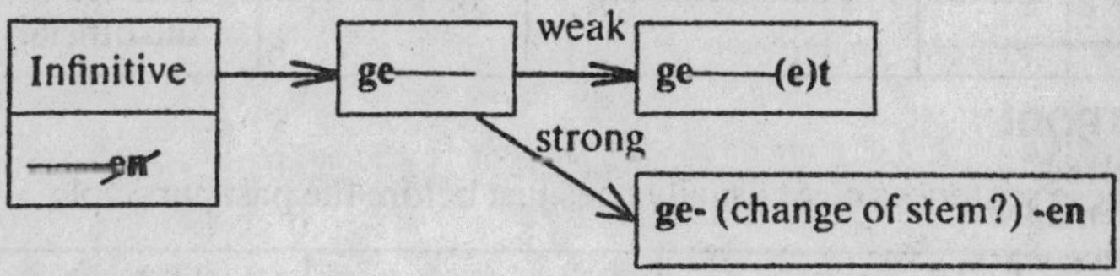

Examples:

1. Weak verbs.

fragen (ask) → **gefragt**
machen (make) → **gemacht**
arbeiten (work) → **gearbeitet**
antworten (answer) → **geantwortet**

2. Strong verbs.

essen (eat) → **gegessen**
fallen (fall) → **gefallen**
stehlen (steal) → **gestohlen**
brechen (break) → **gebrochen**

Sometimes you think that an impossible mouthful like **gearbeitet** can't be right, but it is.

PRACTICE

Write down the meaning and the past participle for each of these verbs:

hören, tragen, nehmen, baden, sehen, helfen, sagen, ziehen, kosten.

Perfect tense word order

The form of **haben** goes in the usual 2nd position in statements and 1st position in questions and the past participle goes to the very end of the sentence. Everything else you want to say is sandwiched in the middle.

ich	**habe**	rest of sentence	**ge——(e)t.**
er/sie/es	**hat**		
wir/sie/Sie	**haben**		**ge—?—en.**

Look at these examples:

Es	**hat**	**den ganzen Tag**	**geregnet.**	It rained all day.
Er	**hat**	**mir den Weg zum Bahnhof**	**gezeigt.**	He showed me the way to the station.
Wir	**haben**	**mit dem Beamten**	**gesprochen.**	We talked to the official.

Negative

In these sentences **nicht** usually goes just before the past participle.

Er	**hat**	**das Auto**	**nicht**	**genommen.**	He didn't take the car.
Ich	**habe**	**meinen Schirm**	**nicht**	**gefunden.**	I didn't find my umbrella.

ANSWERS

to hear, gehört; to carry, getragen; to take, genommen; to bathe, gebadet; to see, gesehen; to help, geholfen; to say, gesagt; to pull, gezogen; to cost, gekostet.

PRACTICE/LEARN BY HEART

Tell somebody what you did yesterday.

1. **Ich habe Pommes frites .....**	I had (ate) some chips.
2. **Ich ... eine Tasse Kaffee .....**	I had (drank) a cup of coffee.
3. **Ich ... ein Buch .....**	I read a book.
4. **Ich ... das Essen .....**	I cooked the meal.
5. **Ich ... mit meinem Chef .....**	I talked to my boss.
6. **Ich ... einen Brief .....**	I wrote a letter.
7. **Ich ... einen Freund .....**	I met a friend.

Verbs which do not add ge-

1. Some verbs do not add **ge-** to the beginning of the past participle because they already have a prefix and they are not separable. If a verb begins with **be- emp- ent- er- ge- ver- zer-** you form the past participle by taking the **-en** ending off the infinitive and adding **-(e)t** for weak verbs and **-en** for strong verbs, together with a possible stem change. Here are some examples:

Weak verbs	*Strong verbs*
bestellen → bestellt	**bekommen → bekommen**
empören → empört	**empfehlen → empfohlen**
enttäuschen → enttäuscht	**entscheiden → entschieden**
gehören → gehört	**gefallen → gefallen**
vermieten → vermietet	**verstehen → verstanden**

The meanings of the above verbs follow in brackets but jumbled up. Can you match them up correctly? (Please, let, hire, anger, recommend, order, decide, understand, belong, get, disappoint)

2. Verbs ending in **-ieren** do not add **ge-** either. They are always weak, so add **-t** in the past participle:

diskutieren → diskutiert **operieren → operiert**

ANSWERS

1. gegessen. 2. habe ... getrunken. 3. habe ... gelesen. 4. habe ... gekocht. 5. habe ... gesprochen. 6. habe ... geschrieben. 7. habe ... getroffen.

REVISION PRACTICE

Write down the past participle of these verbs:
arbeiten, essen, lesen, trinken, kochen, besuchen, telefonieren, schreiben, treffen, fragen, tanzen, verstehen.

Verbs which take *sein*

INTRODUCTION

There is a small group of strong verbs which take **sein** (to be) instead of **haben** when they form the perfect tense. This is a nuisance, but since they are very common verbs you do need to learn them. If you know French, compare them with the verbs which take 'être'. The past participle is formed in exactly the same way as with **haben** and the word order is also unchanged. However, with the negative, **nicht** comes nearer the beginning of the sentence than with **haben**.

HOW TO USE

Ich	**bin**			
Er/sie/es	**ist**	**(nicht)**	rest of sentence	**ge—?—en.**
Wir/sie/Sie	**sind**			

Examples:

Sie	**ist**	**neulich**		**gestorben.**	She died recently.
Wir	**sind**	**nicht**	**zu Fuß**	**gelaufen.**	We didn't go on foot.
Sind	**Sie**	**in Spanien**		**gewesen?**	Have you been to Spain?
Sind	**Sie**	**mit dem Auto**		**gekommen?**	Did you come by car?

ANSWERS

gearbeitet, gegessen, gelesen, getrunken, gekocht, besucht, telefoniert, geschrieben, getroffen, gefragt, getanzt, verstanden.

The German verbs which take **sein** instead of **haben** are:

1. verbs of motion

laufen, kommen, gehen, fahren, fallen, fliegen, schwimmen, reisen, ein/steigen, aus/steigen, um/steigen, an/kommen, ab/fahren, zusammen/stoßen, auf/stehen etc.

2. others

bleiben, sein, werden, sterben.

In a dictionary or word list you will recognise them like this:
laufen (infinitive), **er läuft** (present), **lief** (imperfect), **ist gelaufen** (perfect).

Notice that they are all strong verbs, so take **-en** ending and often change stem. Do spend some time getting familiar with these verbs, as they are difficult to take in and yet are very useful in everyday German. In particular practise:

bleiben	**ich bin ..... geblieben**	I stayed
sein	**ich bin ..... gewesen**	I was/have been
werden	**ich bin ..... geworden**	I have become

LEARN BY HEART

Look up the past participle of the verb at the left of each sentence. Then say what you and your family did last weekend:

1. **fahren**	**Wir ... ans Meer .....**	We went to the seaside.
2. **bleiben**	**Wir ... zu Hause .....**	We stayed at home.
3. **laufen**	**Wir ... im Wald .....**	We walked in the forest.
4. **gehen**	**Wir ... einkaufen .....**	We went shopping.
5. **kommen**	**Wir ... sehr spät nach Hause .....**	We got home very late.

To sum up:

Checklist for using the perfect tense.

1. Start with the infinitive.
2. Check that you do want to use the perfect tense.
3. Is it a weak or a strong verb?
4. Does the past participle take **ge-** at the beginning?
5. If strong, is there a stem change in the past participle?

ANSWERS

1. sind ... gefahren. 2. sind ... geblieben. 3. sind ... gelaufen. 4. sind ... gegangen. 5. sind ... gekommen.

6. Does it take **haben** or **sein**?
7. Is it a separable verb?
8. Remember the word order in the sentence.

You want to say: 'I visited my mother yesterday'.
1. To visit = **besuchen**.
2. It is perfect tense.
3. **Besuchen** is a weak verb.
4. Verbs with **be-** prefix do not take **ge-**.
5. ——
6. Takes **haben**.
7. Not separable.
8. **Haben** in 2nd position, past participle at end.

So you say: **Ich *habe* meine Mutter gestern *besucht*.**

You want to say: 'I walked into town this morning'.
1. To walk = **laufen**.
2. It is perfect tense.
3. **Laufen** is a strong verb.
4. Does take **ge-**.
5. No stem change.
6. Takes **sein**.
7. Not separable.
8. **Sein** in 2nd position, past participle at end.

So you say: **Ich *bin* heute morgen in die Stadt *gelaufen*.**

Pluperfect tense

INTRODUCTION

The pluperfect tense (had done/seen/been etc.) is set one stage further back in time than the perfect or imperfect. It is a direct translation of the English 'had done', 'had gone', etc.

HOW TO USE

The formation of the pluperfect is very similar to the perfect. Instead of the present tense of **haben** or **sein** + past participle, you use the imperfect tense of **haben (hatte/hatten)** or **sein (war/waren)** + past participle:

Ich/er/sie	**war/hatte**	rest of sentence	**ge**——**(e)t** (weak)
Wir/sie/Sie	**waren/hatten**		**ge**—(?)—**en** (strong)

For the small group of verbs which take **sein** see p.23.

You often find the pluperfect used after **nachdem** (after), **bevor** (before), **als** (when).

Future tense

INTRODUCTION

The simplest and most popular way of talking about the future is to use the present tense together with a future time reference, like 'tomorrow', 'next year' etc.

Ich fahre nächste Woche nach München.	I'm going to Munich next week.
In zwei Monaten sind wir wieder zurück.	We'll be back in two months' time.
Wann sind Sie wieder da?	When will you be back?

There is also a real future tense, which is given here mainly for your reference.

HOW TO USE

To form the future tense, use the present tense of the verb **werden** + the infinitive of the verb you want to put in the future. **Werden** is being used as an auxiliary verb, which means that its role is to help form the future tense.

Ich	**werde**	rest of sentence	infinitive of main verb
Du	**wirst**		
Er/sie/es	**wird**		
Wir	**werden**		
Ihr	**werdet**		
Sie/sie	**werden**		

The main verb, the one in the infinitive, goes to the end of the sentence, the present tense of **werden** goes to the normal verb position – 2nd position for statements, 1st position for questions – and the rest of the sentence is sandwiched in the middle.

Examples:

Es	**wird**		**regnen.**	It's going to rain.
Es	**wird**	**heute nachmittag**	**regnen.**	It will rain this afternoon.
Ich	**werde**	**in Berlin Musik**	**studieren.**	I'm going to study music in Berlin.

Important:
Do not confuse 1. the future tense using **werden** with 2. expressions with **wollen** (to want or intend to do something):
Er wird Deutsch studieren. He will study German.
Er will Deutsch studieren. He wants to study German.
There's a world of difference between the two! It's a very tempting mistake for English speakers to make, so be on your guard.

Weak verbs

Weak verbs are regular verbs. If a verb in a dictionary has no distinguishing marks, you can assume that it is weak. All verbs ending in **-ieren** are weak.

Weak verbs follow the rules for all the tenses, so you don't have to worry about stem changes etc.

Strong verbs

INTRODUCTION

Strong verbs are irregular verbs. This means that they act differently from weak or regular verbs. They may have different endings and the stem may change. You can recognise a strong verb in a dictionary because it will have 'ir.' (irregular) after it or there may be an indication of stem change in brackets after the verb: **halten (ä, ie, a)**, to stop.

Next to adjective endings, strong verbs must be the most complicated chunk of German grammar you will have to try to master. Please don't try to learn all the strong verbs in one day or you will go mad. A useful strategy is to learn three or four every day, little and often. The good thing about strong verbs (although you may not think so) is that they are very common, so that when you are in Germany you will constantly hear them in use – and this will help you to learn the correct forms. You won't be able to avoid using them yourself, so it's in your own interest to try and learn them. You will!

Once source of comfort is that you have already mastered one system of strong verbs. English also has strong verbs. You may not have thought about this before, but look at these examples:

find	I have f*ou*nd	stem change just like German strong verbs.
eat	I have eat*en*	-en ending.
write	I have wr*itten*	stem change + -en ending.

Use your knowledge of English to help you learn German strong verbs. You are not starting from scratch!

HOW TO USE

The main times when strong verbs change are:

1. Present tense: **du/er/sie/es** forms often have a stem change.

halten (ä) to stop	**du hältst**	**er hält**
lesen (ie) to read	**du liest**	**er liest**

2. Imperfect tense: all strong verbs have a stem change throughout; the singular has no ending, the plural adds **-en**.

halten (ie)	**der Bus hielt**	**sie hielten**
lesen (a)	**ich las**	**wir lasen**

3. Perfect tense: there is often a stem change in the past participle and the past participle ends in **-en**.

halten (a)	**Der Bus hat gehalten.**
riechen (o) to smell	**Es hat nach Fisch gerochen.**

If you suspect a verb is strong, you want to use it in the perfect tense, and you don't have a dictionary handy, try inventing a 'Germanised' version of the English past participle – and watch the other person's reaction. If it's right, you'll feel very pleased with yourself. If it's wrong, he may still guess your meaning and be able to tell you the correct version.

Separable verbs

INTRODUCTION

Certain verbs in German split into two parts. We have a similar idea in English. We say: I'll *go up* the stairs.
I'll *look* it *up* in the dictionary.
Have you *made* your mind *up*?
Take your shoes and socks *off*.

EXPLANATION

You can often recognise German separable verbs in a word list because there is a stroke (/) between the two parts which separate. The first part of the verb is the prefix and the second part is the real stem of the verb.

These are the most common prefixes you will come across:

ab	**ein**	**nach**	**zu**
an	**fern**	**vor**	**zurück**
auf	**mit**	**weg**	**zusammen**

Verbs which begin with **durch, um, über, wieder** are sometimes separable but not always. See p.32 for details.

You can *hear* that a verb is separable because the prefix is stressed.

You say **éinsteigen** and not **einstéigen**. This is in contrast to other verbs with prefixes which do not separate, which take the stress on the main stem of the verb.

HOW TO USE

Separable verbs can be either strong or weak and can take either **haben** or **sein** in the perfect or pluperfect tense and they follow the usual rules for verbs of that type.

1. Present tense

1. Take off the **-en** ending from the infinitive. 2. Split prefix from main stem. 3. The prefix goes to the end of the sentence. 4. The stem adds the present tense ending. If it's a strong verb, there may be a change of stem. The stem goes to the usual verb position in the sentence.

Infinitive splits	stem+present tense endings		prefix
	Ich ——e		
—/——en	**Er/sie/es ——(e)t**	rest of sentence	—.
	Wir/sie/Sie ——en		

You want to say: 'The train is arriving at half past five tomorrow'. To arrive is **ankommen (an/kommen)**; **der Zug** takes **-t** ending.
Der Zug *kommt* morgen um halb sechs *an*.

You want to ask: 'Do you close as early as 12 o'clock?' To close is **zumachen (zu/machen)**; **Sie** takes **-en** ending. In a question, the verb goes to the first position.
***Machen* Sie schon um 12 Uhr *zu*?**

You want to say: 'The concert begins in quarter of an hour's time'. To begin is **anfangen (an/fangen)**; **das Konzert** takes **-t** ending. **Anfangen** is a strong verb with stem change **a→ä.**
Das Konzert *fängt* in einer Viertelstunde *an*.

2. Imperfect tense

1. Take off the **-en** ending from the infinitive. 2. Split prefix from the main stem. 3. The prefix goes to the end of the sentence. 4. The stem adds **-te** or **-ten** if it is a weak verb. Strong verbs have a stem change + no ending in the singular, add **-en** in the plural. The stem goes to the usual verb position in the sentence.

		1	2	3	4
Infinitive splits	strong	**Ich/er/sie/es**	stem change, no ending	rest of sentence	prefix
		Wir/sie/Sie	stem change, + -en		
—/—~~en~~	weak	**Ich/er/sie/es**	——**te**		
		Wir/sie/Sie	——**ten**		

You want to say: 'He was just closing the window'. To close is **zumachen (zu/machen)**; **machen** is a weak verb, so the **er** form takes **-te** ending.
Er *machte* gerade das Fenster *zu.*

You want to say: 'The conference took place in the Adelphi Hotel'. To take place is **stattfinden (statt/finden)**; **finden** is a strong verb with a stem change from **i→a, die Konferenz** is singular, so the verb has no ending.
Die Konferenz *fand* im Hotel Adelphi *statt.*

3. Perfect tense

HOW TO USE

To form the past participle:
1. Take the **-en** ending from the infinitive.
2. Split the prefix and the main verb.
3. Insert **-ge-** between the prefix and the main verb.
4. Add **-(e)t** ending for weak verbs.

Add **-en** ending for strong verbs, plus possible stem change.

infinitive		split		insert —ge—		add ending
—/—~~en~~	→	——	→	—ge——	→	—ge——(e)t weak —ge-?—en strong

Most separable verbs take **haben**, but some take **sein** (see p.23). The past participle as usual goes to the end of the sentence.

Example:

Wir *haben* viele Leute *kennengelernt*.	We got to know a lot of people.
Sie *haben* noch nicht *aufgemacht*.	They haven't opened yet.
Wann *haben* Sie damit *angefangen*?	When did you start it?
Wir *sind* pünktlich *angekommen*.	We arrived on time.

PRACTICE

Look up your dictionary or verb list and write down a) the past participle and b) whether the following verbs take **haben or sein**: **abschleppen** (to tow away); **aufhören** (to stop); **zumachen** (to close); **anziehen** (to put on clothes); **anrufen** (to phone); **aussteigen** (to get out of vehicle); **ankommen** (to arrive).

LEARN BY HEART

Choose the right verb from this list, put it into the perfect tense, then complete the following questions which you might find useful when you want some information:

zumachen einkaufen anrufen ankommen abfahren

1. … **Frau Schmidt schon** …..?	Has Frau Schmidt phoned?
2. … **der Zug schon** …..?	Has the train already left?
3. … **Sie schon** …..?	Have you already been shopping?
4. … **der Laden schon** …..?	Has the shop already closed?
5. … **der Zug aus Braunschweig**…..?	Has the train from Braunschweig arrived?

ANSWERS

1. Practice

abgeschleppt, aufgehört, zugemacht, angezogen, angerufen + haben
ausgestiegen, angekommen + sein

2. Learn by heart

1. Hat … angerufen. 2. Ist … abgefahren. 3. Haben … eingekauft. 4. Hat … zugemacht. 5. Ist … angekommen.

4. Pluperfect tense

The pluperfect tense follows exactly the same pattern as the perfect tense, except that instead of the present tense of **haben** and **sein**, you use the imperfect.

ich/er/sie/es	**hatte / war**
wir/sie/Sie	**hatten / waren**

5. After modal verbs and *werden* (future tense)

The modal verb (see p.34 for details) or the form of **werden** goes to the usual main verb position and the separable verb goes to the end of the sentence and is in the infinitive, so it does not split.

1	2	3	4
Ich	**werde/möchte/** etc.		**—/——en.**
Er/sie/es	**wird/möchte/**	rest of sentence	infinitive of separable verb
Wir/sie/Sie	**werden/möchten**		

Ich *möchte* meine Familie *anrufen*. I'd like to phone my family.
Wann *werden* Sie in Frankfurt *ankommen*? When will you arrive in Frankfurt?

EXPLANATION

Unfortunately the prefixes **um- durch- über-** and **wieder-** sometimes indicate a separable verb and sometimes not. There is no easy way to tell which one is separable – you have to keep your eyes and ears open. The separable verbs will have the stress on the prefix, whereas the verbs which don't separate will have the stress on the stem. Here are a few common examples:

separable	*not separable*
úm/ziehen (to move house)	**umgéhen** (to avoid)
dúrch/fahren (to travel through)	**durchdénken** (to think something through)
wiéder/sehen (to see again)	**wiederhólen** (to repeat)

LEARN BY HEART

You are talking to a friend who is going to Berlin. Using the verbs from the list at the bottom, write down what you would say in German.

1. What time did you get up today? **Wann ... Sie heute .....?**
2. When does your train leave? **Wann ... Ihr Zug?**
3. When are you coming back? **Wann ... Sie .....?**
4. What time do you arrive in Berlin? **Um wieviel Uhr ... Sie in Berlin .....?**
5. Who's picking you up at the station? **Wer ... Sie vom Bahnhof .....?**
6. When will you phone me? **Wann ... Sie mich .....?**

abholen, abfahren, anrufen, aufstehen, zurückkommen, ankommen

Separable verbs are used a lot in everyday conversation. Here are a few farewell messages you might hear. The English translations have been mixed up. Can you match the correct English sentence to the German one?

1. **Geben Sie nicht zuviel Geld aus!** A. Come back soon!
2. **Kommen Sie gut an!** B. Phone us next week!
3. **Kommen Sie bald wieder!** C. I hope you arrive safely.
4. **Ruhen Sie sich gut aus!** D. Don't spend too much money!
5. **Rufen Sie uns nächste Woche an!** E. Have a good rest!

Notice that in the imperative (commands) the verb goes to the first position and the prefix goes to the end of the sentence.

ANSWERS

1st exercise

1. sind ... aufgestanden; 2. fährt ... ab; 3. kommen ... zurück; 4. kommen ... an; 5. holt ... ab; 6. rufen ... an.

2nd exercise

1. D; 2. C; 3. A; 4. E; 5. B.

Modal verbs

INTRODUCTION

When dealing with other people it's important to be polite and appreciative. Modal verbs ('can', 'should', 'have to', etc.) help you, for example, to make polite requests or offer help to someone and are especially effective when combined with **bitte**, **danke** or **entschuldigen Sie** (excuse me). They provide you with a much more sophisticated way of giving orders than simply using the imperative. Look at the difference between 'Bring me another piece of bread' (imperative) and 'Could you please bring me another piece of bread?'. 'Could' is a modal verb and it turns the order into a request.

It's worth taking the trouble to learn and practise these verbs because you can combine them with hundreds of other verbs to make lots of different sentences. They will be invaluable to you in shops, banks, going to the theatre – whenever you are in contact with German people.

EXPLANATION

The nice thing about modal verbs is that there are only two forms for each tense. To form the singular of the present tense, take off the **-en** from the infinitive. There may be a change of stem and there is no ending. The plural form of the present tense is exactly the same as the infinitive:

Infinitive				
	→	**Ich/er/sie/es** no ending + possible stem change	→	**will**
wollen		**Wir/sie/Sie** same as infinitive		**wollen**

Here is a complete list of the modal verbs:

	müssen must	**dürfen** may	**können** can	could	**wollen** want to	**sollen** shall	**mögen** would like to
ich er sie es	**muß**	**darf**	**kann**	**könnte**	**will**	**soll**	**möchte**
wir sie Sie	**müssen**	**dürfen**	**können**	**könnten**	**wollen**	**sollen**	**möchten**

HOW TO USE

Modal verbs cannot stand on their own because the meaning of the sentence would be incomplete. They are always used with a second verb. When using the present tense, the modal verb goes to the usual verb position (see p.51) and the second verb goes to the end of the sentence and is in the infinitive:

Ich/er/sie/es	**muß**	rest of sentence	infinitive of 2nd verb
Wir/sie/Sie	**müssen**		

Look at these examples:

Ich *muß* jetzt nach Hause *gehen*.	I have to go home now.
Wir *möchten* jetzt *bestellen*.	We'd like to order now.
***Kann* ich mit einem Scheck *bezahlen*?**	Can I pay by cheque?

You will soon get into the habit of putting the second verb at the end – very often German people will finish the sentence for you! People will still understand you if you put the second verb in the middle of the sentence but you will sound very English because the rhythm is wrong.

LEARN BY HEART

1. Here are some very polite expressions which will help you to get what you want without offending other people:

Ich möchte zahlen/ein Zimmer bestellen/Plätze reservieren.	I'd like to pay/book a room/reserve seats.
Darf ich hier rauchen/parken?	May I smoke/park here?
Muß ich lange warten?	Do I have to wait long?
Könnten Sie mir bitte helfen?	Could you please help me?
Könnten Sie mir bitte sagen/zeigen ...?	Could you please tell/show me ...?
Könnten Sie das bitte wiederholen/buchstabieren?	Could you please repeat/spell that?
Könnten Sie etwas lauter/leiser/langsamer sprechen?	Could you please speak a bit louder/softer/more slowly?

2. Offers of help:

Kann ich Ihnen helfen?	Can I help you?
Soll ich Sie um sieben Uhr wecken?	Would you like me to wake you at seven o'clock?

3. Suggestions:

Wollen wir in die Stadt fahren?	Shall we go into town?
Wir könnten ins Theater gehen.	We could go to the theatre.
Möchten Sie das Museum sehen?	Would you like to see the Museum?
Ich kann den Film wirklich empfehlen.	I can really recommend the film.

EXPLANATION

Some notes about individual modal verbs:

1. **wollen** = to want to

N.B. **Ich will** does not mean 'I will' (future). See future tense, p.25.

Wollen + nicht indicates unwillingness to do something and can be strong enough to mean outright refusal to do something.

Das will ich doch nicht machen.
I don't want to do it/I'm not going to do it.

The imperfect tense of **wollen** is:

ich/er/sie/es	**wollte** = wanted
wir/sie/Sie	**wollten** = wanted

2. **Möchte/möchten** = would like (to)

There is no verb **möchten**. These forms are a part of the verb **mögen** = to like, but they are used just like modal verbs. It is important to recognise the difference in tone between saying:

Ich will ein Stück Kuchen.	I want a piece of cake. (a bit rude)
Ich möchte ein Stück Kuchen.	I'd like a piece of cake. (much more polite)

Try not to confuse **ich möchte** (I would like) and **ich wollte** (I wanted).

3. **Können** = to be able to

kann/können = can　　**könnte/könnten** = could

4. **Müssen/dürfen**

Ich muß = I must, I have to
Ich darf = I may, I am allowed to.
But contrary to what you might expect,
Ich muß nicht = I don't have to (literally 'I don't must').

Sie müssen nicht vorher anrufen.	You don't have to phone in advance.

Sie können eine Flasche Wein bringen, Sie müssen aber nicht. You can bring a bottle of wine, but you don't have to.

If you want to say 'mustn't', use **dürfen + nicht** or **kein**:
Sie dürfen nicht hineingehen. You mustn't go in.
Ich darf kein Fett essen. I mustn't eat any fat.

5. **Sollen**
This is a rather strange verb. It is tempting to translate it by 'shall', but there's more to it than that. Look at these examples:

Ich soll morgen um 10 Uhr am Flughafen sein. I am to be/ am supposed to be/ am expected to be at the airport at 10 o'clock tomorrow.
Es soll in Südfrankreich sehr warm sein. It's supposed to be/ They say it's very warm in the South of France.
Um wieviel Uhr soll ich kommen? When shall I/ am I to/ would you like me to come?
Soll ich Ihnen einen Tee machen? Shall I/ would you like me to make you a cup of tea?

In other words, you can sometimes use 'shall' to translate **sollen** but you must be clear that underlying **sollen** is often the idea that a third person has to give his consent or that the information is dependent on a third person. There is often an idea of duty or obligation to someone other than the speaker.

Similarly in the imperfect tense, **sollte/sollten** can mean 'should', but also means 'ought to, was expected to, was supposed to'.

LEARN BY HEART
You have been invited out to dinner with friends. Choose the correct verb to give you some useful expressions.

1. **Sollte/Könnte ich bitte das Salz haben?** Could I have the salt, please?
2. **Kann/Möchte ich Ihnen helfen?** Can I help you?
3. **Muß/Darf ich rauchen?** May I smoke?
4. **Möchte/Könnte ich ein Glas Wasser bekommen?** Could I have a glass of water?

5. **Ich muß/darf keine Milchprodukte essen.**	I'm not allowed to eat any dairy products.
6. **Ich muß/darf leider jetzt gehen.**	I'm afraid I'll have to go now.
7. **Könnten/Sollten Sie mir bitte sagen, wo die Toilette ist?**	Could you please tell me where the toilet is?

MODAL VERBS IN THE PAST

Although there is a perfect tense for modal verbs, it is much more common to use them in the imperfect. To form the imperfect, take **-en** from the infinitive and add **-te** or **-ten**. There is often a change of stem too. People often get confused using the imperfect of modal verbs because they use Umlauts wrongly. In the imperfect tense of modal verbs *there are no Umlauts*.

wollen	**ich wollte/Sie wollten**	wanted to
müssen	**ich mußte/Sie mußten**	had to
können	**ich konnte/Sie konnten**	was/were able to
sollen	**ich sollte/Sie sollten**	ought to/should/was expected to
dürfen	**ich durfte/Sie durften**	was/were allowed to

The word order is the same as for the present tense.

Ich *mußte gehen.*	I had to go.
Wir *konnten* nicht *sehen.*	We couldn't see.
Er *sollte* jetzt da *sein.*	He ought to be there by now.

Perfect tense

Use **ich habe** etc. as for any perfect tense, but instead of using a past participle the modal verb stays in the infinitive and comes after the other verb at the very end of the sentence.

Present tense: **Das kann ich machen.**	I can do it.
Perfect tense: **Das *habe* ich *machen können.***	I was able to do it.

That's when the real fun starts, piling up all the verbs at the end of the sentence!

ANSWERS

1. Könnte; 2. Kann; 3. Darf; 4. Könnte; 5. darf; 6. muß; 7. Könnten.

Note:

Ich wollte = I wanted to **Ich konnte** = I was able to	**Ich möchte** = I would like to **Ich könnte** = I could
Imperfect (no Umlaut)	Subjunctive (Umlaut)

Reflexive verbs

INTRODUCTION

Reflexive verbs are verbs which seem to 'come back on themselves'. They are used to describe actions or feelings which are important to the speaker personally. The nearest thing we have in English is the use of 'myself', 'yourself' etc. with a verb:
I addressed myself to the problem.
Can you let yourself in?
Make yourself at home, etc.

I addressed myself

The circular movement revolving around the verb emphasises the personal nature of the verb.

HOW TO USE

In order to use reflexive verbs in German you use the verb in the normal way, taking into consideration tense, type of verb etc., but in addition you add an extra reflexive pronoun which is the equivalent of 'myself', 'yourself' etc. The reflexive pronoun usually goes into the 3rd position in the sentence, sticking very closely to the verb. The German reflexive pronouns are:

ich → mich	**wir → uns**
du → dich	**ihr → euch**
er/sie/es → sich	**sie/Sie → sich**

How can you tell that a verb is reflexive? In the infinitive you see: **sich irren** or **s. irren.**

1. Present tense

ich irre mich	I am mistaken	**wir irren uns**	we are mistaken
du irrst dich	you are mistaken	**ihr irrt euch**	you are mistaken
er irrt sich	he is mistaken	**sie irren sich**	they are mistaken
sie irrt sich	she is mistaken	**Sie irren sich**	you are mistaken

Question
Irren Sie sich? Are you mistaken?

2. Imperfect tense

The word order is exactly the same as for the present tense. The reflexive pronouns are exactly the same. The verb takes imperfect tense endings and stem changes.

3. Perfect tense

1	2	3	4	5
personal pronoun	**haben/sein**	reflexive pronoun	rest of sentence	past participle
Ich **Er**	**habe** **hat**	**mich** **sich**	 **nicht**	**geirrt.** **geirrt.**

Question

Haben	**Sie**	**sich**		**geirrt?**

Here are some common reflexive verbs:

sich aus/ruhen	to have a good rest	**sich setzen**	to sit down
sich ärgern	to get angry	**sich beeilen**	to hurry up
sich erinnern	to remember	**sich waschen**	to get washed

HOW TO USE

In the examples so far, the reflexive pronoun has been accusative (see p.85): **mich, sich** etc.

There is a second type of reflexive verb in which the reflexive pronoun is dative (see p.89): **mir, dir, sich** etc. Look at these examples:

Ich habe *mir* die Zähne geputzt. I cleaned my teeth.

Ich kann *mir* im Moment kein Auto leisten.	I can't afford a car at the moment.
Er wollte *sich* die Nachrichten ansehen.	He wanted to have a look at the news.

In all these examples the reflexive pronoun means either: 'your', 'my' etc.; as in 'I cleaned *my* teeth' (i.e. to myself); or 'to/for myself, yourself' etc., as in 'to have a look (for himself) at the news'.

The dative pronouns for reflexive verbs are:

mir	**uns**
dir	**euch**
sich	**sich**

so there is only a difference where the **mir** and **dir** forms occur. All the rest are the same as for the accusative. Still, the difference is important because it involves a different idea of relationships.

Some common verbs of this type are:

sich etwas leisten	to afford something
sich etwas ansehen/anschauen	to have a look at something
sich etwas kaufen	to buy oneself something
sich etwas überlegen	to think something over
sich die Haare waschen	to wash one's hair

LEARN BY HEART

Here are some sentences which are useful for personal conversations. Choose the correct reflexive pronoun to insert in each blank.

1. **Ich habe … geirrt.**	I've made a mistake.
2. **Es tut mir leid, ich kann … nicht erinnern.**	I'm sorry, I can't remember.
3. **Er hat … so geärgert!**	He was so angry!
4. **Guten Tag, ich möchte … anmelden.**	Good morning, I'd like to register.
5. **Ich muß … die Haare waschen.**	I'll have to wash my hair.
6. **Interessieren Sie … für Musik?**	Are you interested in music?
7. **Wir freuen … auf Ihren Besuch.**	We look forward to your visit.
8. **Bitte setzen Sie …**	Please sit down.
9. **Das muß ich … noch überlegen.**	I'll have to think it over.

ANSWERS

1. mich; 2. mich; 3. sich; 4. mich; 5. mir; 6. sich; 7. uns; 8. sich; 9. mir.

Imperative

INTRODUCTION

There are several levels of giving commands, depending on how friendly, polite etc. your relations are to the other person.

HOW TO USE

The straightforward imperative form (i.e. command form) in German is the same as the present tense but the verb goes into the 1st position:

1 2 **Gehen Sie!**	Go!
1 2 3 **Kommen Sie hierher.**	Come here!
1 2 3 **Trinken Sie Ihren Kaffee aus.**	Drink up your coffee!

But you won't get very far if you order people about like that. In order not to offend people you often have to cushion your command:

1. With words like **bitte**.

Gehen Sie bitte durch.	Please go straight through.
Kommen Sie bitte ins Vorderzimmer.	Please come into the front room.
Hören Sie bitte.	Please listen.
Gucken Sie mal.	Have a look here.

2. Or you could be even less abrasive and use modal verbs (see p.34):

Könnten Sie bitte leiser sprechen?	Could you please speak more softly?

Your command is phrased as a polite request, the other person is made to feel he is doing you a favour.

Wollen wir ins Kino gehen?	Shall we/ let's go to the cinema?

3. The infinitive (see p.168) is used especially for instructions, e.g. on packets and labels as well as in public notices and loudspeaker announcements:

Hier öffnen	Open here
Hier schneiden	Cut here
Bitte weitergehen	Move along please
Bitte sofort einsteigen	Please get into (vehicle) at once
Türen schließen	Shut the doors

Here are a few more – can you guess what they mean?

1. **Nicht stören!**
2. **Geld einwerfen!**
3. **Bitte zurücktreten!**
4. **Karten hier entwerten!**
5. **Zimmerschlüssel abgeben!**
6. **Rauchen einstellen!**

Sein

The imperative form of **sein** is: **Seien Sie**. You can use it if you want to fall over backwards not to offend someone when asking them to do something:

Seien Sie bitte so nett.	Would you be so kind?

Negative commands

To the foreigner the most important commands often take the form of regulations or notices telling you something is forbidden. The vocabulary is also often difficult to guess. Here are a few examples:

Kein Zutritt		No entry, no access
Kein Durchgang		No way through
Kein Trinkwasser		Not drinking water
Keine Durchfahrt		No through road
Das Rauchen/Das Spielen auf dem Rasen/Das Autowaschen etc.	**ist untersagt** **ist nicht gestattet** **ist verboten** **ist streng verboten** **ist nicht erlaubt**	Smoking/Playing on the grass/Washing your car is forbidden!
Sie dürfen hier nicht parken/zelten/kochen/waschen/ etc.		You're not allowed to park/camp/cook/wash here.

ANSWERS

1. Do not disturb. 2. Insert money. 3. Please step back. 4. Stamp tickets here. 5. Hand in your room key. 6. Extinguish your cigarette.

LEARN BY HEART

Here are a few imperatives which you might find useful in social situations:
Try to fill in the correct form of the verb. Choose four of the six verbs below.

1. **..... Sie bitte herein.**	Please come in.
2. **..... Sie bitte Platz.**	Do sit down.
3. **Entschuldigen Sie, das Rauchen ist hier nicht .....**	Excuse me, you're not allowed to smoke here.
4. **..... wir heute abend in die Stadt fahren?**	Shall we go into town tonight?

nehmen gestattet verboten kommen wollen könnten

Subjunctive

INTRODUCTION

This grammar is not really the place to go into all the details of the German subjunctive, but many of you will have heard of the term and may be a bit confused about it. I have tried to reduce the subjunctive to its bare bones, to what is really useful for everyday use.

ANSWERS

1. Kommen. 2. Nehmen. 3. gestattet. 4. Wollen.

EXPLANATION

Up till now in this book, we have been looking at verbs in very concrete, real settings. The subjunctive is a form of the verb which introduces a certain distance from reality, sometimes an element of doubt or wishful thinking. It is used for example:

1. When reporting what someone else has said.

Er sagte, sie *wäre* zum Flughafen gefahren.	He said she'd gone to the airport.

Because you are relying on what he said, you can't be absolutely sure that she really did go to the airport. So 'had gone' is subjunctive: **wäre gefahren**.

2. When translating English 'if'.

Confusingly, the German word for 'if' is **wenn**. The word 'if' introduces an element of unreality or wishful thinking into the sentence:

Wenn ich ein reicher Mann *wäre* ...	If I were a rich man ...

But I'm not and probably never will be. The English word 'were' in this sentence is a leftover form of the old English subjunctive and expresses the uncertainty caused by 'if'.

3. When translating English 'would/could'.

a) Making polite requests:

***Könnten* Sie mir bitte ... zeigen?**	Could you please show me ...?
***Würden* Sie bitte so nett sein ...?**	Would you be so kind as to ...?
***Würden* Sie bitte die Tür zumachen?**	Would you please shut the door?

b) Reacting very politely to other people:

Das *wäre* nett.	That would be lovely.

c) Making suggestions:

Wir *könnten* nach Mexiko fahren.	We could go to Mexico.
An Ihrer Stelle *würde* ich ...	If I were you I would ...

d) Expressing wishes:

Ich *würde* gern mal nach Australien fahren.	I'd love to go to Australia.

4. Some everyday expressions which make conversation and dealings in banks, shops etc. pleasant and civilised.

***Könnten* Sie das bitte einpacken?**	Could you wrap it up please?
***Könnte* ich das bitte anprobieren?**	Could I try this on please?
Das *müßte* reichen/ gehen.	That ought to be enough/ be OK.
Das *wäre* nett.	That would be lovely/ nice.
Danke, das *wäre* es.	Thank you, that's all for now.
Ich *hätte* gern + noun	I'd like ...
Ich *würde* gern + infinitive	I'd like to ...

HOW TO USE

Infinitive	*Subjunctive*			
haben	**ich/er/sie/es**	**hätte**	**wir/sie/Sie**	**hätten**
sein		**wäre**		**wären**
können		**könnte**		**könnten**

Please note the Umlaut throughout. In fact in these examples above the subjunctive form is exactly the same as the imperfect tense except for the Umlaut. To translate 'would', you generally use **würde/würden** + infinitive.

Ich *würde* meine Stelle *kündigen.*	I'd hand in my notice.
Er *würde* nach Amerika *fahren.*	He'd go to America.
***Würden* Sie so freundlich *sein*?**	Would you be so kind?

Putting it all together

Here are a few examples of the subjunctive which you might find useful:

1. In conversation:

Wenn ich die Zeit *hätte, würde* ich gern mehr Deutsch *lernen.*	If I had the time, I would love to learn more German.
Wenn ich die Wahl *hätte, würde* ich zu Hause *bleiben.*	If I had the choice, I would stay at home.
Wenn ich so jung *wäre, würde* ich eine Weltreise *unternehmen.*	If I were as young as that, I'd go on a trip round the world.

2. In business letters:

Ich *wäre* Ihnen sehr dankbar, wenn Sie mir Ihre Broschüre zuschicken *könnten*.	I would be very grateful if you could send me your brochure.

There is more to the subjunctive than this, and if you are interested in taking it further it is better to consult a more specialised grammar book.

Passive

INTRODUCTION

You use the passive when you don't want to be specific about who was/is doing the action.

EXPLANATION

If I say: 'John kicked the ball over the fence', I am being quite specific about who did the action. But if I say: 'The ball was kicked over the fence', I leave open the identity of the kicker. The form 'was kicked' is passive. So the passive is really a different way of describing the same event. The emphasis is on the action itself and is deflected away from the person doing the action.

This can often be very useful if you want to spotlight the action or keep the identity of the doer vague. The Germans are very fond of using the passive and you will hear and see it a lot more than in English. You do not have to learn it yourself, because there is a simpler alternative using **man** (one, people in general), see p.102. However, it is certainly useful to be able to recognise the passive.

HOW TO USE

1. Present tense

Use the present tense of **werden** (p.25) which goes to the usual verb position (see p.51) + the past participle (p.19) of the main verb which goes to the end of the sentence. The rest of the sentence is sandwiched in the middle.

1	2	3	4
Ich	**werde**		**ge——(e)t.** weak
Er/sie/es	**wird**	rest of sentence	
Wir/sie/Sie	**werden**		**ge—(?)—en.** strong

Sie *werden erwartet*.	You're expected./They're expecting you. ('They' not specified.)
Nein danke, ich *werde abgeholt*.	No thanks, I'm getting a lift./I'm being met. (You don't want to be specific about who is meeting you.)
Das Haus *wird* gerade *gebaut*.	The house is (in the process of) being built.

2. Imperfect tense

Use the imperfect tense of **werden (wurde/wurden)** + the past participle:

Ich/er/sie/es	**wurde***	rest of sentence	**ge——(e)t.** weak
Wir/sie/Sie	**wurden***		**ge—(?)—en.** strong

*N.B. no Umlaut!

Er *wurde* gestern *operiert*.	He was operated on yesterday.
Wir *wurden* vom Bahnhof *abgeholt*.	We were picked up from the station.
Die Kirche *wurde* im 16. Jahrhundert *gebaut*.	The church was built in the 16th century.

There are two important points which often confuse people:

1. **Werden** *does not have an Umlaut* in the passive. Many people think it does because they confuse **wurde/wurden** with **würde/würden** (=would), see p.46.

2. Many people ask: what's the difference between
Das Geschäft *ist* geschlossen and
Das Geschäft *wird* geschlossen?

You can say both, but they mean different things. If you use **sein** with a past participle, you are describing a state of affairs. The shop is closed. It's a description of the shop, just as you could say the shop is big or small or expensive. The word **geschlossen** is being used here just as any other adjective. If you use **werden** with the past participle, you are describing the act of closing the shop. **Das Geschäft wird geschlossen** means that the shop is being closed. In your mind's eye you can see the action taking place.

Ihr Wagen ist repariert.	Your car is repaired, i.e. it is OK now, it is in a repaired state.
Ihr Wagen wird repariert.	Your car is being repaired, i.e. the repairing is going on now.

This problem is difficult for English speakers because we use 'to be' to form our own passive.

3. Perfect tense

This looks quite complicated, but you can survive without learning it
Use the present tense of **sein** (to be) + past participle of main verb + **worden.**

1	2	3	4	5
Ich	**bin**		**ge——(e)t**	
Er/sie/es	**ist**	rest of sentence	**ge—(?)—en**	**worden.**
Wir/sie/Sie	**sind**			

1	2	3	4	5	
Ihr Auto	**ist**	**gestern**	**repariert**	**worden.**	Your car was repaired yesterday.
Mein Bruder	**ist**	**in der Klinik**	**operiert**	**worden.**	My brother was operated on in the clinic.
Meine Handtasche	**ist**		**gestohlen**	**worden.**	My handbag has been stolen.

In most cases you can use the imperfect just as well as the perfect for actions in the past.

EXPLANATION

A word of warning: many people confuse **worden** (which is used only in the perfect tense of the passive) with **geworden** (which is *not* used in the passive). **Geworden** is the past participle of **werden** (to become).

Sentence structure

INTRODUCTION

If you can master German word order and sentence structure you will sound much more German than someone who gets all the endings right but still sticks to English word order. German is a very logical language and the rules about word order are very straightforward. They may seem a lot to take in at one time, but persevere and you will astonish yourself. Train your ear to listen to how German people structure their sentences and always try to copy them. Train yourself to predict what is coming at the end of the sentence. This will help you to think ahead and will stop you being preoccupied with English word order – which won't be of much help to you.

EXPLANATION

I am going to distinguish between two types of sentence: simple sentences and complex sentences.

1. Simple sentences

In simple sentences (i.e. sentences which contain only one verb) which are statements (i.e. not questions or commands) the most important rule is that the main verb always goes into the 2nd position. This does not mean that it is the 2nd word in the sentence because the 1st position may be occupied by a phrase consisting of several words.

1	2	3	
Die Tür	**ist**	**auf.**	The door is open.

Die Tür is a unit forming in this example the subject of the verb. The verb **ist** is in 2nd position, i.e. the 2nd unit in the sentence. Here are some more examples:

1	2	3	
Wir	**fliegen**	**morgen nach Hause.**	We're flying home tomorrow.
Meine Tante	**besucht**	**uns nächste Woche.**	My aunt is visiting us next week.

In these examples the first unit is the subject (i.e. does the action), the second unit is the verb and the rest of the sentence (expressions of time or place etc.) comes afterwards.

This is the usual sentence structure which we have in English. We nearly always begin a sentence with the subject, followed by the verb, followed by the object. Most other phrases get attached to the end of this core sentence, and expressions of time can choose to go before or after the subject-verb-object core.

Yesterday	I went to see my friend in Brixton.	
	I went to see my friend in Brixton	yesterday.

German sentence structure is much more flexible. You can begin a sentence with almost anything you like: the subject, the object, an expression of time or place, the dative and many other expressions. Take a sentence like:

Ich fahre nächste Woche mit meiner Tante nach Amerika. I'm going to America next week with my aunt.

You can say:

1	2	3	4	5
Ich	**fahre**	**nächste Woche**	**mit meiner Tante**	**nach Amerika.**
Nächste Woche	**fahre**	**ich**	**mit meiner Tante**	**nach Amerika.**
Nach Amerika	**fahre**	**ich**	**nächste Woche**	**mit meiner Tante.**
Mit meiner Tante	**fahre**	**ich**	**nächste Woche**	**nach Amerika.**

Another example:

Der Mann	**hat**	**mein Auto**	**genommen.**
Mein Auto	**hat**	**der Mann**	**genommen.**

N.B. the main verb is *always* in the 2nd position.

How can you start a sentence with virtually any type of word and still avoid total confusion? How can you tell who did the action and who was on the receiving end of it? The answer lies:

1. With the verb. The second position is an anchor point around which the rest of the sentence floats. The verb ending can already tell you a lot about who did the action.

2. With the well-defined system of endings for words which accompany nouns (**der/die/das, ein/kein/mein** etc. see pp.94, 97). This is where the time and trouble spent in learning nominative, accusative etc. endings is repaid handsomely because it enables you to tell whether the car took the man or the man took the car.

Mein Auto hat der Mann genommen.

It's tempting to assume that **Mein Auto** is the subject, but look at **der Mann. Der** words only take **der** in the nominative, so **der Mann** must be the subject. Of course, commonsense tells you that it must be that way round, but you'd be surprised how often people get it wrong.

Although I said earlier that the rest of the sentence seems to float around the verb in the 2nd position, the parts which float do not just appear in any position they happen to fancy. Within the floating structure there are strict rules of word order:

1. Expressions of time (=when) must come before expressions of manner (=how), which must come before expressions of place (=where).

2. Pronouns must come before nouns.

3. If there are two nouns together, the nominative must come before the dative, which must come before the accusative.

4. If there are two pronouns together, the nominative must come before the accusative, which must come before the dative.

German sentence structure:

1	2	3
Nominative Accusative Dative Time Manner Place etc.	verb	rest of sentence. Rules: 1) time 2) manner 3) place 1) pronouns 2) nouns two nouns: 1) Nom 2) Dat 3) Acc two pronouns: 1) Nom 2) Acc 3) Dat

Still looking at simple statements, here are some examples with other tenses and verb constructions:

1. Perfect tense

1	2	3	4
	haben/sein	rest of sentence	past participle
Mein Onkel **In dem Lokal**	**ist** **haben**	**neulich** **wir Steaks**	**gestorben.** **gegessen.**

2. Modal verbs / **werden** (future tense) / **würde/würden** (=would)

1	2	3	4
	modal/ werden	rest of sentence	infinitive of 2nd verb
Ich	**möchte**	**meine Schwester**	**anrufen.**
Nächste Woche	**werde**	**ich meinen Geburtstag**	**feiern.**
Das	**würde**	**ich so gern**	**machen.**

3. Passive
a) Present and imperfect tenses

1	2	3	4
	werden	rest of sentence	past participle of 2nd verb
Nach dem Krieg	**wurde**	**Deutschland**	**geteilt.**
Die Wohnung	**wird**	**einmal in der Woche**	**geputzt.**

b) Perfect tense

1	2	3	4	5
Meine Schuhe **Wir**	**sind** **sind**	**schon** **um sieben Uhr**	**geputzt** **geweckt**	**worden.** **worden.**

4. Separable verbs
a) Present and imperfect tenses

1	2	3	4
Er	**bat**	**mir sein Auto**	**an.**
Ich	**kaufe**	**immer bei Horten** (=name of store)	**ein.**

b) Perfect and pluperfect tenses

1	2	3	4
Sein Auto	**hat**	**er mir**	**angeboten.**
Er	**war**	**schon**	**wegegangen.**

5. Simple questions and commands
To form simple questions or commands, you put the verb in the 1st position and the subject* usually (but not always) goes in the 2nd position.

1	2	3
Fahren	**Sie**	**bitte etwas langsamer!**
Geben	**Sie**	**mir bitte den Schlüssel!**
Fahren	**Sie**	**immer so schnell?**
Haben	**Sie**	**gut geschlafen?**
***Hat**	**Ihnen**	**das Essen geschmeckt?**
Ist	**das Haus**	**schon geputzt worden?**
Möchten	**Sie**	**in den Garten gehen?**
Haben	**Sie**	**viele Leute kennengelernt?**

Questions using question words (when? where? etc.)

1	2	3	4
question word	verb	subject *(usually)	rest of sentence

There is no room left for manoeuvre in the 1st position because it is occupied by the question word, so the subject or other word from the 1st position is shunted further down.

1	2	3	4
Wie lange	**haben**	**Sie**	**Deutsch studiert?**
Wann	**sind**	**Sie**	**nach Deutschland gekommen?**
***Wie**	**hat**	**Ihnen**	**das Essen geschmeckt?**

*The questions marked with an asterisk are examples of the subject (**das Essen**) not occupying its expected position. The reason for this is the rule which says that pronouns (**Ihnen**) must come before nouns (**das Essen**) in the rest of the sentence which comes after the verb (see p.53).

2. Complex sentences

In a complex sentence (i.e. a sentence with more than one main verb), each section of the sentence is focussed upon a particular verb. We call these sections *clauses*. In the following examples the beginning and end of a clause is shown by a stroke (/) and the verb upon which it is focussed is written in italics.

/He *told* me/ that he *would phone* at eight o'clock/.
/I *am* not sure/ whether it *is going* to rain today/.
/He *kissed* her goodbye,/ then *walked away* quickly/ and *was lost* in the crowd/.

In German the beginnings and endings of clauses are always clearly signposted by commas. The commas must be there and are part of the grammatical structure of the sentence. There are several types of complex sentences because there are several sets of rules about word order, depending on the construction used.

1. Verb stays in the usual position (2nd for statements, 1st for questions/commands).
a) After **und** (and), **aber** (but), **oder** (or), **sondern** ('but' after negative statement), **denn** (because).

1 2
Bleiben Sie hier, oder kommen Sie lieber mit?
Are you staying here or do you want to come along too?

1 2
Wir können entweder bei uns zu Hause essen, oder wir können zu den Italienern gehen.

We can either eat at home or go out to the Italian restaurant.

Wir waren heute am Strand, aber es[1] war[2] eigentlich zu kalt zum Schwimmen.
We went to the beach today but it was really too cold to swim.

N.B. **und, aber** etc. are connecting words *between* clauses. They do not occupy a word-order position in the clause which follows them.

Er kommt nicht? Das kann ich schon verstehen, denn er[1] wohnt[2] sehr weit von hier.
He's not coming? I can well understand that because he lives a long way away from here.

b) In the shortened form of indirect speech and expression of opinions. (N.B. no word for 'that'.)

Ich finde,	**das**	**ist sehr nett von ihm.**	I think it's very nice of him.
Ich meine,	**er**	**ist schon weg.**	I reckon he's already gone.
Ich glaube,	**er**	**kommt nicht.**	I think he's not coming.

2. Verb stays in the 2nd position, but there is no room in the 1st position because it is occupied already by words like **dann** (then) and **also** (so). This forces all other parts of the sentence to come after the verb. The subject therefore normally occupies the 3rd position.

Wir sind zu Karstadt gegangen, dann[1] waren[2] wir[3] bei Hertie, dann[1] sind[2] wir[3] in die Konditorei gegangen. Dort haben wir ein Stück Kuchen gegessen, dann[1] wollten[2] wir[3] ins Kino gehen. Das Kino war zu, also[1] sind[2] wir[3] nach Hause gefahren. Ich hatte meinen Schlüssel vergessen, also mußten[2] wir[3] draußen warten.

We went to Karstadt*, then we were in Hertie*, then we went to the cake shop. We had a piece of cake there, then we wanted to go to the cinema. The cinema was closed, so we went home. I had forgotten my keys, so we had to wait outside.

You can either start a completely new sentence with **dann/also** or you can add a comma at the end of the previous clause and continue in the same sentence.

3. The verb is sent from its 2nd position to the very end of the clause. This word order occurs:

a) After **daß** (that), **weil** (because), **obwohl** (although), **damit** (so that), **wenn** (if) etc. They are all words which introduce clauses which can not stand on their own – these are known as subordinate clauses.

N.B. This overrides any other word order rules which affect the sentence.

1	2	3	4
	verb		

Modal verbs move from the 2nd position to come after the 2nd verb infinitive.

1	2	3	4	5
	modal verb		infinitive	

For separable verbs: the stem moves from 2nd position and joins up with the prefix at the end of the sentence:

1	2	3	4
	stem		prefix+stem.

In the perfect tense, **haben/sein** move from the 2nd position to come after the past participle:

1	2	3	4	5
	haben/sein		past participle	

*Department stores in Germany.

Wir freuen uns, *daß* Sie gekommen *sind.*	We are pleased that you came.
Uns hat keiner gesagt, *daß* das Autowaschen hier verboten *ist.*	Nobody told us that you're not allowed to wash your car here.
Ich bin etwas später gekommen, *weil* ich mich zuerst anmelden *mußte.*	I arrived a bit late because I had to register first.
Ich möchte nicht, *daß* Sie zuviel Geld *ausgeben.*	I don't want you to spend too much money.
Wir haben ihn nicht gesehen, *weil* er um die Ecke gewartet *hat.*	We didn't see him because he was waiting round the corner.
Er kommt heute nicht mit, *weil* sein Geld alle *ist.*	He's not coming with us today because he's run out of money.

Notice the comma which comes before **daß/weil/wenn** etc. This is an essential point of German grammar indicating the end of one clause and the beginning of the next. It is *not* a piece of decoration to be put in or left out at will.

b) In relative clauses (with 'who'/'which'/'that')

Wo ist das Buch, *das* Sie in der Hand *hatten*?	Where's the book (which) you had in your hand?
Das war der längste Film, *den* ich je gesehen *habe.*	That was the longest film (which) I've ever seen.
Ich habe gestern mit dem Mann gesprochen, *der* unser Auto repariert *hat.*	I spoke yesterday to the man who repaired our car.

c) In indirect questions (e.g. 'I don't know where he is'. The direct question is: 'Where is he?' The indirect question is contained within the sentence and is introduced by a question word).

Könnten Sie mir bitte sagen, *wo* die Toiletten *sind*?	Could you please tell me where the toilets are?
Wissen Sie zufällig, *wann* dieser Zug in Basel *ankommt*?	Do you happen to know when this train arrives in Basel?
Ich habe keine Ahnung, *wer* die Hauptrolle im Film gespielt *hat.*	I've no idea who played the lead in the film.
Ich weiß nicht, *ob* das *stimmt.*	I don't know if that's right.

d) After **als** ('when' in the past), **nachdem** (after), **wenn** ('when' in the present and future), **bevor** (before), **seit** (since), **während** (while), **bis** (until). These are all expressions of time. They follow the same word order pattern as a), b) and c) but the time clause can come either at the beginning of the sentence or later on in the sentence. Notice what happens to the word order in the other clause:

Time clause at beginning of sentence	Other clause: verb in 1st position
Als wir wegfahren wollten,	**hat** (1) **es** (2) **gegossen.**
Just as we were about to depart, it poured down.	
Bevor Sie sich entscheiden,	**sollten** (1) **Sie** (2) **unbedingt die Broschüre lesen.**
Before you make up your mind, you ought to read the brochure.	

Other clause first: normal word order	Time clause 2nd
Ich habe viel gelesen,	**als ich zwanzig war.**
I read a lot	when I was twenty.
Wir haben schnell ein Bier getrunken,	**bevor wir zum Bahnhof gegangen sind.**
We had a quick beer	before we went to the station.

Now look at each of the above examples in a), b), c) and d) very carefully and note down 1. what type of verb it contains and 2. what tense the verb is in. Check again with the explanation at the beginning of each section and see if you can work out why the word order is as it is.

4. The verb in one clause is in the infinitive.
a) After **um ... zu** (in order to)
The infinitive goes to the end of its clause. Separable verbs insert **-zu-** between the prefix and the main stem:

First clause	Second clause			
	um	rest of clause	zu	infinitive
Wir sind etwas früher gekommen,	**um**	**Ihnen**	**zu**	**helfen.**
Ich brauche etwas,	**um**	**die Dose**		**aufzumachen.**

b) After certain verbs which are followed by **zu**, e.g. **vergessen** (to forget), **versuchen** (to try), **auf/hören** (to stop), **an/fangen** (to start), **empfehlen** (to recommend) etc.

Ich habe vergessen, ihn zu fragen. I forgot to ask him.
Er hat mir empfohlen, den Intercity-Zug zu nehmen. He recommended I take the Intercity train.

LEARN BY HEART

In the sentences below the verbs have been taken out of position. Rewrite the German sentences with the verbs in the correct position. The verbs are underneath the sentence, and are in the wrong order.

1. **Ich Sie nicht, weil es zu spät.** / **angerufen, war, habe** — I didn't phone you because it was too late.
2. **Ich, wo wir ihn.** / **kennengelernt, habe, haben, vergessen** — I've forgotten where we met him.
3. **Sie Lust, jetzt in die Stadt zu?** / **haben, fahren** — Do you feel like going into town now?
4. **Ich nicht, ob die anderen schon zu Hause.** / **sind, weiß** — I don't know whether the others are already home.

5. **Ich mein Studium, weil ich kein Geld.** **aufgeben, hatte, mußte**	I had to give up my studies because I had no money.
6. **Ich mit meinem Bruder ins Krankenhaus, dann wir mindestens eine Stunde.** **gewartet, bin, haben, gegangen**	I went with my brother to the hospital and then we waited for at least an hour.

ANSWERS

1. Ich *habe* Sie nicht *angerufen*, weil es zu spät *war*. 2. Ich *habe vergessen*, wo wir ihn *kennengelernt haben*. 3. *Haben* Sie Lust, jetzt in die Stadt zu *fahren*? 4. Ich *weiß* nicht, ob die anderen schon zu Hause *sind*. 5. Ich *mußte* mein Studium *aufgeben*, weil ich kein Geld *hatte*. 6. Ich *bin* mit meinem Bruder ins Krankenhaus *gegangen*, dann *haben* wir mindestens eine Stunde *gewartet*.

Questions

INTRODUCTION

You will find yourself having to answer many questions and you will want to ask many questions yourself. Questions are quite straightforward in German. There are several types:

HOW TO USE

1. Simple questions expecting a 'yes/no' answer.

To form this type of question you simply swop over the word order of a normal statement so that the verb comes in the first position and the subject of the verb goes into the second position.

Statement	*Question*	
Er hat lange gewartet.	**Hat er lange gewartet?**	Did he wait long?
Er wohnt in Paris.	**Wohnt er in Paris?**	Does he live in Paris?
Sie kommen aus Berlin.	**Kommen Sie aus Berlin?**	Do you come from Berlin?

Notice that there is no German word for 'do/does/did' – it is absorbed into the verb.

Of course not all statements begin with the subject of the sentence. You might have a statement like:

Gestern hat er seine Mutter besucht. He visited his mother yesterday.

To make this into a question, the verb has to go in the first position, the subject goes into the second position, so **gestern** is shunted further down the question:

1 2 3 1 2 3

Hat er gestern seine Mutter besucht? or **Hat er seine Mutter gestern besucht?**

2. Use of **nicht wahr?** (isn't it/aren't you? etc.)
If you are expecting the answer 'yes', you can save yourself the trouble of forming a question. Instead you say your normal statement, then tack on **nicht wahr?** to the end, and you have a question expecting the other person to agree with you. **Nicht wahr?** means 'isn't that so?'.

Das Essen schmeckt gut, nicht wahr?	The food's good, isn't it?
Sie sind Fräulein Schmidt, nicht wahr?	You're Fräulein Schmidt, aren't you?
Sie wohnen in Kiel, nicht wahr?	You live in Kiel, don't you?
Der Bus fährt um acht Uhr, nicht wahr?	The bus leaves at 8 o'clock, doesn't it?

3. Use of question words (who? when? where? etc.)
The word order when using question words is:

1	2	3	4
question word	verb	subject (usually)	rest of question
Was **Wann**	**haben** **wollen**	**Sie** **wir**	**heute gemacht?** **essen?**

Sometimes the subject can not come in the third position because there is another rule of word order which says that in the part of the sentence which comes after the verb, pronouns must come before nouns (see p.53). So, if the subject is a noun and there is another pronoun after the verb, the subject gets shunted further down the line:

1	2	3	4
Wie	**hat**	**Ihnen** (pronoun)	**das Essen geschmeckt?** (subject)

The most common question words are:
Wann? = when?

Wann fahren wir?	When are we leaving?

Wieviel? = how much/how many?

Wieviel Zigaretten haben Sie noch?	How many cigarettes have you got left?

Wo? = where?

Wo sind hier die Toiletten?	Where are the nearest toilets?

Wohin? = where to?

Wohin fahren Sie?	Where are you going (to)?

Woher? = where from?

Woher kommen Sie?	Where do you come from?

Wer? = who?

Wer? changes its ending depending on whether it is nominative, accusative, dative or genitive. It takes the same endings as **der** (see p.94).

Nom.	**wer?**	who?
Acc.	**wen?**	whom?
Dat.	**wem?**	(to/with etc.) whom?
Gen.	**wessen?**	whose?

Wer ist jetzt an der Reihe?	Who is next?
Für wen ist der Brief?	Who is the letter for? (for whom?)
Wem gehört der Koffer?	Who does the case belong to? (to whom?)

Note:

1. Many English people confuse **wer?** (=who) and **wo?** (=where). Try to get this clear in your own mind – it is the opposite way round from what you might expect.
2. Make sure you pronounce **wen?** (=whom?) with a long **e** (sounds like English 'vein') and **wenn?** (=when?) with a short **e** (sounds like the 'e' in English 'when'). Otherwise nobody will understand you.

Wie? = how?

Wie geht es Ihnen?	How are you?
Wie sagt man das auf Deutsch?	How do you say that in German?
Wie alt sind Ihre Kinder?	How old are your children?

Welcher/welche/welches? = which?
Welcher is an adjective (see p.112 Situation type 4).

Welches Zimmer haben Sie?	Which room do you have?
In welchem Zimmer sind Sie?	Which room are you in?
Welche Größe nehmen Sie?	Which size do you take?

Warum? = why?

Warum haben Sie das gemacht?	Why did you do it?

Was? = what?

Was ist das?	What's this?
Was kostet das?	How much is this? (What does it cost?)

PRACTICE/LEARN BY HEART

A. Questions you might hear:

Wie ist Ihr Name?	What is your name?
Woher kommen Sie?	Where do you come from?
Was sind Sie von Beruf?	What do you do for a living?
Was kann ich für Sie tun?	What can I do for you?
Was möchten Sie?	What would you like?
Haben Sie gut geschlafen?	Did you sleep well?
Hat Ihnen das Essen geschmeckt?	Did you enjoy your meal?

B. Questions you might want to ask:

Was kostet das Zimmer?	How much is the room?
Kann ich hier telefonieren?	Can I make a phone call here?
Sprechen Sie Englisch?	Do you speak English?
Wo ist hier eine Bank?	Where is there a bank round here?
Wann fährt der Zug nach Basel?	When does the train for Basel leave?
Wie heißen Sie?	What is your name?
Könnten Sie mir bitte helfen?	Could you please help me?
Wie sagt man 'spaniel' auf Deutsch?	How do you say 'spaniel' in German?
Was ist das?	What's this?

HOW TO USE

You can also form question words with prepositions. You add **wo-** to the beginning of the preposition. If the preposition begins with a vowel, you add **wor-**.

Worüber sprechen Sie?	What are you talking about?
Wofür ist das?	What is this for?
Wovon hängt das Ergebnis ab?	What does the result depend on?

Was für? = what kind of?

Was für eine Stadt ist das?	What kind of a town is this?
Was für Leute sind das?	What sort of people are they?

Negatives

INTRODUCTION

There is an art to saying no. It can be embarrassing not knowing how to say 'no' in a foreign language.

HOW TO USE

1. No

The simple word for 'no' is **nein**. But it is not always appropriate on its own. If somebody says to you:

Möchten Sie eine Tasse Kaffee? Would you like a cup of coffee?

it would be very rude to decline with **Nein**, so here are some helpful expressions to buffer your refusal.

If somebody offers you something you don't want, say

Nein danke or
Danke or
(Nein) Vielen Dank
= No thank you.

If they insist and you still want to decline:

Nein danke + give a reason (e.g. **Ich muß fahren./Ich habe keinen Hunger** etc.)

Nein, wirklich nicht!	No thank you, I really don't want to.
Das ist sehr nett von Ihnen, aber + reason	That's very kind of you, but ...
Es tut mir leid, aber + reason	I'm sorry but ...

You can express regret by using:

Es tut mir leid.	I'm sorry.
Leider ...	Unfortunately . . .
Wir haben leider keine Zimmer frei.	I'm afraid we have no rooms.
Das Hotel ist leider ausgebucht.	I'm afraid the hotel is fully booked.
Es tut mir leid, aber ich kann nicht.	I'm sorry but I can't.

It can be awkward trying to refuse an invitation. It's clearly better to give some kind of reason so that the other person doesn't feel offended. On the other hand, you are not obliged to tell them all the details of your private life or the real reason why you wish to refuse. The polite but firm way to refuse an invitation is to say:

Nein danke, ich bin schon verabredet.	No thank you, I'm already committed elsewhere.

or

Es tut mir leid, ich habe schon etwas vor.	I'm sorry but I'm busy then.

You don't need to go into any more detail.

2. Not + verb Use 'nicht'.

Ich weiß es nicht.	I don't know.
Ich habe das Haus nicht gefunden.	I didn't find the house.
Bitte rauchen Sie nicht.	Please don't smoke.

Notice that there is no word for 'don't/didn't'. That is the English way of making the negative and it is unnecessary in German.

Nicht likes to stay close after the verb in 2nd position, but if there is a subject (nominative), object (accusative) or indirect object (dative) coming after the verb, **nicht** is shunted further down the sentence. Look at the following examples:

a) **Nicht** stays close to the verb in 2nd position:

Ich bin nicht müde.	I'm not tired.
Ich habe nicht sehr gut geschlafen.	I didn't sleep very well.

b) **Nicht** is shunted further down the sentence:

Er hat mir die Fotos nicht gezeigt.	He didn't show me the photos.
Geht es Ihrem Mann nicht gut?	Is your husband unwell?
Gefällt Ihnen die Bluse nicht?	Don't you like the blouse?

You can also add **nicht-** as a prefix to nouns, like 'non-' in English.
der Nichtraucher non-smoker (carriage in train etc.)

3. 'No not ... any/ not ... a' + noun. Use 'kein'.

EXPLANATION

Kein is a sort of negative article. An exact equivalent does not exist in English, and English people find it tricky to use. The most important thing is to study the examples carefully and try to learn them by heart. Above all, if you catch yourself about to say **nicht ein** for 'not a' – STOP! It is not German. **Nicht ein** can not exist in German – it must be replaced by **kein**.

HOW TO USE

Like the definite article (**der/die/das**) and the indefinite article (**ein/eine/ein**), **kein** also takes endings which are related to:

1. whether the noun it accompanies is singular or plural;
2. which **der/die/das** group the noun belongs to;
3. what role the noun plays in the sentence (=case).

The endings are exactly the same as the endings for **ein** (see p.97).

	der group	**die** group	**das** group	plural
Nom.	no ending	**-e**	no ending	**-e**
Acc.	**-en**	**-e**	no ending	**-e**
Dat.	**-em**	**-er**	**-em**	**-en**

Examples:

Es gibt hier keine Luft.	There's no air in here./There isn't any air in here.
Wir haben heute keine Tomaten.	We haven't any tomatoes today./We have no tomatoes today.
Ich habe keine Ahnung.	I have no idea.
Er spricht kein Deutsch.	He doesn't speak any German.
Ich habe kein deutsches Geld.	I haven't any German money./I have no German money.

LEARN BY HEART

Go back over the examples with **nicht** and **kein** then decide how to put these sentences into German. Remember, if you find yourself writing **nicht ein** or **nicht** + noun, STOP AND THINK AGAIN!

1. I can't speak German.
2. I'm not hungry.
3. I don't understand.
4. I'm sorry, I don't know.
5. I can't pick you up from the station.
6. I haven't any time.
7. I'm sorry, that's not possible.
8. Aren't you tired?
9. There's no beer in the fridge.
10. Don't you eat any meat?

4. Nobody / not ... anybody = niemand

Ich sehe niemand.	I can't see anyone.
Hier ist niemand.	There isn't anybody here.

5. Nothing / not ... anything = nichts

English people often have difficulty connecting 'nothing' with 'not ... anything'. It's tempting to look up the word 'anything' in the dictionary and add **nicht** to it, but that's not German. The way to say 'not ... anything' is **nichts**. And **nichts** is a very different word from **nicht** (='not'+verb).

Ich verstehe nicht.	I don't understand.
Ich verstehe nichts.	I don't understand anything.
Ich weiß nicht.	I don't know.
Ich weiß nichts.	I don't know anything.
Ich habe noch nichts gegessen.	I haven't had anything to eat yet.
Danke, ich möchte nichts trinken.	No thank you, I don't want anything to drink.

6. Nowhere / not ... anywhere = nirgends or nirgendwo

Er ist nirgends zu finden.	He can't be found anywhere.
Ich habe ihn nirgends gesehen.	I haven't seen it/him anywhere.

ANSWERS

1. Ich spreche kein Deutsch. 2. Ich habe keinen Hunger. 3. Ich verstehe nicht. 4. Es tut mir leid, ich weiß es nicht. 5. Ich kann Sie nicht vom Bahnhof abholen. 6. Ich habe keine Zeit. 7. Es tut mir leid, das geht nicht. 8. Sind Sie nicht müde? 9. Es gibt kein Bier im Kühlschrank. 10. Essen Sie kein Fleisch?

7. Never/not ... ever = nie or niemals or noch nie

Ich fahre nie ohne Gürtel.	I never drive without my seat belt fastened.
Ich habe nie Tee mit Milch getrunken.	I've never drunk tea with milk.
Ich war noch nie in meinem Leben betrunken.	I've never been drunk in my life.
Wir waren noch nie in der Schweiz.	We've never been to Switzerland.

8. Not ... yet = noch nicht + verb/ noch kein + noun

Ich kann mich noch nicht entscheiden.	I can't make up my mind yet.

9. Neither ... nor = weder ... noch

Weder ich noch meine Freundin wird da sein.	Neither I nor my friend will be able to come.

Conjunctions

INTRODUCTION

'Conjunction' means 'joining together'. Conjunctions are words which join two parts of a sentence together (e.g. 'and', 'but', 'so' etc.). If you say, 'The dress is red and blue', the word 'and' is a conjunction joining the two colours. You can also use conjunctions to join clauses (longer sections of a sentence which contain a verb). You can alter the tone of your sentence by choosing different conjunctions:

Clause 1	*Conjunction*	*Clause 2*
We went to the beach	and but because although when	it was raining.

HOW TO USE

The most important thing to know about German conjunctions is that when they join two clauses together they often affect word order.

1. Simple conjunctions

These do not affect word order:

Und (and), **aber** (but), **oder** (or), **denn** (for, because) etc.

klein *aber* fein	small but fine
mit *oder* ohne Sahne	with or without cream
Wir sind in die Wirtschaft gegangen *und* haben ein Bier getrunken.	We went into the pub and had a beer.
Wir haben einen Picknick gemacht, *aber* es war sehr kalt.	We had a picnic but it was very cold.

2. Conjunctions which affect word order

a) Inversion of subject and verb. When you use these conjunctions, the subject and the verb swop positions so that the verb goes into the 1st position and the subject goes into the 2nd position. **Also** (so – N.B. **also** never means English 'also'); **dann** (then); **sonst** (otherwise); **deshalb** (therefore, for that reason) etc.

Ich muß jetzt gehen, *sonst* komme ich zu spät.	I'll have to go now. Otherwise I'll be late.
Ich möchte ein Paar Schuhe kaufen, *deshalb* will ich morgen früh in die Stadt fahren.	I'd like to buy a pair of shoes, which is why I want to go to town early tomorrow morning.
Wir haben Tee getrunken, *dann* sind wir spazieren gegangen.	We had some tea, then we went for a walk.

b) The verb is sent to the end of its clause.
Time – **nachdem** (after); **bevor** (before); **seit/seitdem** (since); **als** (when); **wenn** (when); **bis** (until); **während** (while) etc.
N.B. use **als** for 'when' in the past and **wenn** for 'when' in the present and future.
Reason – **da** (since); **weil** (because).
Objection – **obwohl** (although); **trotzdem** (in spite of that) etc.
If – **wenn** (if); **falls** (if, in case).
Purpose – **damit** (so that); **so ... daß** (so that)
daß (that)
ob (whether).

Sie müssen warten, *bis* der Zug *hält*.	You have to wait till the train stops.
Stimmt es wirklich, *daß* er sehr krank *ist*?	Is it really true that he is very ill?
Wissen Sie, *ob* Herr Schweik jetzt zurück *ist*?	Do you know whether Herr Schweik is back now?
Man muß lange warten, *wenn* man ein Paket aufgeben *will*.	You have to wait a long time if you want to send a parcel.
Kinder dürfen hier nicht schwimmen, *weil* das Wasser sehr tief *ist*.	Children are not allowed to swim here because the water is very deep.

Notice that there is always a comma before the conjunction if it introduces a new clause. In English, we often don't bother with a comma but in German it must be there to indicate the end of one clause and the beginning of another.

Nouns

General Information

INTRODUCTION

Nouns in German are always written with a capital letter.

Every noun belongs to one of three groups:

masculine	*feminine*	*neuter*
der	**die**	**das**

The terms masculine, feminine and neuter are a bit misleading because you find objects such as 'table' (**der Tisch**) belonging to the **der** group, and 'bus stop' (**die Haltestelle**) belonging to the **die** group. How can you tell which group a noun belongs to? Even Germans don't know every one. In a dictionary you will often see n.m. (for **der** group), n.f. (for **die** group) or n.n. (for **das** group). But you can't always go around with your nose in a dictionary so here are some rules which will help you.

EXPLANATION

The following nouns are usually in the **der** group:
- Nouns ending in **-er** which describe a person's job: **der Verkäufer** (salesman); **der Kellner** (waiter) etc.
- Nouns referring to a male person: **der Mann** (man); **der Onkel** (uncle); **der Vater** (father); **der Junge** (boy); **der Polizist** (policeman) etc.

The following nouns are usually in the **die** group:
- Nouns ending in **-in**, which is the female ending for a person's job: **die Studentin** (female student); **die Verkäuferin** (saleslady); **die Reiseleiterin** (female courier) etc.
- Nouns referring to a female person: **die Mutter** (mother); **die Frau** (woman); **die Tante** (aunt) etc.

– Nouns ending in **-ung**: **die Quittung** (receipt); **die Rechnung** (bill); **die Zeitung** (newspaper); **die Abteilung** (department); **die Heizung** (heating); **die Bedienung** (service); **die Übernachtung** (overnight stay); **die Verpflegung** (board, meals) etc.
– Nouns ending in **-heit**: **die Krankheit** (illness) etc.
– Nouns ending in **-keit**: **die Staatsangehörigkeit** (nationality) etc.
– Nouns ending in **-e**: **die Sprache** (language); **die Speisekarte** (menu); **die Steckdose** (electric socket); **die Stunde** (hour) etc.
– Nouns ending in **-schaft**: **die Botschaft** (embassy) etc.
– Nouns ending in **-tät**: **die Spezialität** (speciality); **die Elektrizität** (electricity) etc.
– Abstract ideas: **die Jugend** (youth); **die Ruhe** (peace, tranquility) etc.
– Nouns ending in **-bahn**: **die Autobahn** (motorway); **die Straßenbahn** (tram) etc.
– Nouns ending in **-tion** or **-sion**: **die Koalition** (coalition); **die Situation**; **die Rezeption**; **die Konfession** (religion) etc.

The following nouns are usually in the **das** group:
– Foreign words imported, e.g. from English or French: **das Restaurant**; **das Taxi**; **das Büro** (office); **das Hotel**; **das Parfüm** etc.
– Nouns ending in **-chen**: **das Mädchen** (girl); **das Brötchen** (bread roll); **das Würstchen** (small sausage) etc.
– Nouns ending in **-lein**: **das Fräulein** (girl) etc.
– Latin words: **das Studium** (period of study), **das Museum** etc.

Does it matter if you make a mistake with these groups? Yes and no. No, if you only want to try and get across simple messages. Provided your pronunciation is clear enough people will understand you even if you get the **der/die/das** wrong. Yes, if you want to speak reasonably correct German. It is important to know which group a noun belongs to because this affects many other grammar items, such as pronouns (p.99) and adjective endings (p.110). It also helps to avoid misunderstandings. But remember the golden rule: it's more important to say *something* even if it's wrong than to say nothing because you can't remember whether it should be **der**, **die** or **das**. Germans will appreciate you making the *effort*!

LEARN BY HEART

Whenever you meet a new noun, look it up in the dictionary and write down which group it belongs to. Try to learn the nouns which crop up again and again.

Here are some nouns you will need when looking for accommodation in Germany. Sort them out into three groups (**der/die/das**) and write the English meaning next to them:
1. **Campingplatz**. 2. **Hotel**. 3. **Gasthaus**. 4. **Frühstück**. 5. **Jugendherberge**. 6. **Empfang**. 7. **Formular**. 8. **Übernachtung**. 9. **Zimmer**. 10. **Parkplatz**.

Now try to learn them by heart.

Here are the names of some well-known German newspapers and magazines. Fill in the **der/die/das** and write down the English meaning:
1. **Spiegel**. 2. **Bildzeitung**. 3. **Welt**. 4. **Abendblatt**. 5. **Zeit**.

Plural forms

INTRODUCTION

Just as in English we say 'one m*a*n' but 'two m*e*n' and 'one guitar' but 'two guitar*s*', so in German the plural form of a noun is often different from the singular form. In addition, **der/die/das** changes to **die** for all three groups:

EXPLANATION

These are the main types of change together with the way they are shown in dictionaries:

ANSWERS ·
1st exercise
1. der (campsite). 2. das (hotel). 3. das (guest house). 4. das (breakfast). 5. die (youth hostel). 6. der (Reception). 7. das (form)! 8. die (overnight stay). 9. das (room). 10. der (car park).
2nd exercise
1. der (mirror). 2. die (picture newspaper). 3. die (world). 4. das (evening paper). 5. die (time).

	Dictionary
– Add **-n** or **-en** or **-nen**:	
Frau → Frauen	**Frau** *n.f.* (**-en**)
Freundin → Freundinnen	**Freundin** *n.f.* (**-nen**)
– Change a vowel sound by adding an Umlaut (**ä, ö, ü**):	
Garten → Gärten	**Garten** *n.m.* (¨)
Apfel → Äpfel	**Apfel** *n.m.* (¨)
– Don't change anything at all:	
Kellner → Kellner	**Kellner** *n.m.* (–)
Schlüssel → Schlüssel	**Schlüssel** *n.m.* (–)
– Add **-er**, usually with an Umlaut (ä, ö, ü):	
Haus → Häuser	**Haus** *n.n.* (¨**er**)
Glas → Gläser	**Glas** *n.n.* (¨**er**)
– Add **-e**, often with an Umlaut (ä, ö, ü):	
Fahrplan → Fahrpläne	**Fahrplan** *n.m.* (¨**e**)
Tag → Tage	**Tag** *n.m.* (**-e**)
– Add **-s**:	
Bar → Bars	**Bar** *n.f.* (**-s**)
Ticket → Tickets	**Ticket** *n.n.* (**-s**)

How do you know how to form the plural of a new noun? Unfortunately there's no easy answer. Most **die** group nouns form the plural by adding **-n** or **-en**. Some **das** group nouns (foreign words) add **-s**. Does it really matter? Only up to a point. Try to learn the plural form of new nouns when you look up the **der/die/das** information and make a special effort to memorise the nouns you keep coming across. It really is a question of memorising and practice.

SURVIVAL

If you don't know the plural:

1. Stop and look up your phrase book, or
2. Try **-en** or **-er** on the end of the noun and see how the other person reacts. If they still don't understand, say the singular, e.g. **ein Kind** and then say **Wie sagt man, zwei was?** (How do you say two of them?).

N.B. Certain words which are singular in English are always plural in German:

a headache	**Kopfschmerzen**
a toothache	**Zahnschmerzen**
pain	**Schmerzen**
hair	**Haare**
furniture	**Möbel**

Others are plural in English but always singular in German:

clothes	**die Kleidung**
trousers	**die Hose**
glasses (spectacles)	**die Brille**
scissors	**die Schere**

LEARN BY HEART

Here are some nouns you might need when talking about your family or going out shopping. Use your dictionary to find the plural forms and write them down, together with the English meaning.

1. **Mann**	4. **Kind**	7. **Taxi**	10. **Bus**
2. **Apfel**	5. **Mantel**	8. **Tomate**	11. **Kartoffel**
3. **Kaufhaus**	6. **Glas**	9. **Fahrkarte**	12. **Geschäft**

Now cover them up and learn by heart.

Here are some signs you will nearly always see in the plural. Can you match the English words to the German?

1. **Zigaretten**	4. **Liköre**	7. **Lebensmittel**
2. **Damen**	5. **Herren**	8. **Toiletten**
3. **Möbel**	6. **Streichhölzer**	9. **Spirituosen**

liqueurs/ matches/ toilets/ spirits/ Ladies/ furniture/ Gentlemen/ food/ cigarettes/

ANSWERS

1. Männer (men) 2. Äpfel (apples) 3. Kaufhäuser (department stores) 4. Kinder (children) 5. Mäntel (coats) 6. Gläser (drinking glasses) 7. Taxis (taxis) 8. Tomaten (tomatoes) 9. Fahrkarten (tickets) 10. Busse (buses) 11. Kartoffeln (potatoes) 12. Geschäfte (shops)

1. cigarettes 2. Ladies 3. furniture 4. liqueurs 5. Gentlemen 6. matches 7. food 8. Toilets 9. spirits

Cases

INTRODUCTION

In English, nouns are quite simple. Usually the only thing you have to bother about is adding -s for the plural. But in German, nouns have four different *cases*.

Case refers to the role of a particular noun or pronoun in a particular sentence. You may never have thought about nouns or pronouns having different roles unless you have studied grammar at some point.

If you take a sentence like: '*John* wanted *me* to give *him* an *apple*', you can see that there are several nouns or pronouns in this sentence. If we try to replace 'John' with a pronoun we could say: '*Him* wanted to give me an apple', or '*He* wanted to give me an apple'. But one of these is wrong. Similarly we don't say: 'John wanted *I* to give *he* an apple'. Why not?

The reason these versions are wrong is that 'I' and 'he' can only play a certain role in a sentence. We say that 'I' or 'he' must be the *subject* of the sentence, in other words the person *doing* the action. Similarly 'me' or 'him' cannot be the subject of the sentence. They are on the *receiving* end of the action (or the verb). We say that 'him' or 'me' must be the *object* of the sentence. In English, the subject usually comes before the verb and the object comes after it.

Furthermore, we make a difference between different kinds of object, the *direct object* and the *indirect object*.

What John said was: 'Give me the apple'. Here we have two objects: 'me' and 'the apple'. Which one does John want? – 'the apple'. We call this the *direct object*. We call 'me' the *indirect object* because John really means: 'Give (to) me the apple'.

When looking at German grammar, these three different roles, subject, direct object and indirect object are called *cases*.
The subject corresponds to the nominative case;
the direct object corresponds to the accusative case;
the indirect object corresponds to the dative case;
and there is one more: the genitive case, which is used for possession, e.g. 'my brother's house' etc.

In English we only notice the different cases when using pronouns such as I/me or he/him. But in German you notice the cases with nouns as well. The fact that a noun is in for example the dative or the accusative case will affect the endings of words which usually accompany nouns:
- **der/die/das** (definite article, see p.94);
- **ein/kein** (indefinite article, see p.97);
- **mein/Ihr/sein/ihr** etc. (possessive adjectives, see p.120);
- adjectives, see p.110

as well as the words which replace nouns:
- pronouns, see p.99.

N.B. usually the noun itself does not change. You use the form you find in the dictionary. However, there are a few common nouns which add **-n** or **-en** in all cases except the nominative singular:

der Student (-en)	student
der Bauer (-n)	farmer
der Junge (-n)	boy
der Name (-n)	name
der Herr (-n)	gentleman

HOW TO USE
To find out more, look up nominative, accusative, dative and genitive, where each case is explained in full. If you want to see an overall picture of German case endings, check with the section on patterns (p.161).

Nominative case

INTRODUCTION
Nominative describes the role of a particular noun or pronoun in a particular sentence.

WHEN TO USE
Nouns are in the nominative case:

1. when they are *doing* the action, i.e. when they are the *subject* of the verb. Look at these examples. The noun in the nominative case is in italics.

***Das Telefon* klingelt.**	The phone is ringing.
***Peter* raucht eine Zigarette.**	Peter's having a cigarette.
***Die Deutschen* essen viel Schweinefleisch.**	The Germans eat a lot of pork.
Da drüben liegt *meine Tasche*.	My bag's over there.
Gestern ist *meine Schwester* gekommen.	My sister arrived yesterday.
Wo wohnt *Ihre Mutter*?	Where does your mother live?

From these examples it is clear that the noun in the nominative case is not automatically at the beginning of the sentence as it usually is in English, so it is sometimes a bit tricky to work out who did what to whom! The clue is to look for the signs:

a) verb ending – tells you whether the subject is singular or plural and which person (he/you/they etc);
b) **der/die/das** form or **ein/kein/mein/Ihr** form also gives information about singular/plural and case;
c) use your commonsense! The cigarette didn't smoke Peter.

2. After verbs like **sein** (to be) and **werden** (to become) in which the person before and after the verb are one and the same, e.g. **Mein Bruder ist Ingenieur. Mein Bruder** and **Ingenieur** are one and the same person so both are in the nominative case.

EXPLANATION

If a noun is in the nominative case, you use the form you find in the dictionary for either singular or plural. The accompanying words look like this:

NOMINATIVE ENDINGS

Singular			*Plural*	
der group (*no ending*)	die group (-e *ending*)	das group (*no ending*)	all groups (-e *ending*)	
der	**die**	**das**	**die**	the
ein	**eine**	**ein**	—	a/an
kein	**keine**	**kein**	**keine**	no/not…any
mein	**meine**	**mein**	**meine**	my
Ihr	**Ihre**	**Ihr**	**Ihre**	your

Help yourself to learn: can you spot the *pattern* of endings?

PRONOUNS

Pronouns are used to replace nouns and therefore can also be in the nominative case. If a pronoun is doing the action, is the subject of the verb, it looks like this:

Singular			*Plural*		
ich	(I)		**wir**	(we)	
er	(he/it)	to replace **der** words			
sie	(she/it)	to replace **die** words	**sie**	(they)	to replace **die** plural
es	(it)	to replace **das** words			
Sie	(you)		**Sie**	(you)	

PRACTICE/LEARN BY HEART

In order to ask about other people's families etc. you need the nominative case and a few basic verbs such as: **sein** (to be), **haben** (to have), **arbeiten** (to work), **wohnen** (to live), **kommen** (to come), **gehen** (to go). Can you underline the nominative words in these statements and questions?

1. **Das ist mein Mann.** This is my husband.
2. **Er ist Beamter.** He is a civil servant.
3. **Wir wohnen in Birmingham.** We live in Birmingham.
4. **Wir haben drei Kinder.** We have three children.
5. **Was sind Sie von Beruf?** What do you do (for a living)?

Now fill in the blanks about yourself and learn the questions and information by heart.

1. .... **ist** (your name). *My name is* (your name).
2. ... **bin** (your job). *I am a* (your job).
3. ... **komme aus** (your town). *I live in* (your town).
4. .... **arbeitet in** (town). *My husband/wife etc. works in* (town).

ANSWERS

1st exercise

1. Das, mein Mann 2. Er, Beamter 3. Wir 4. Wir 5. Sie

2nd exercise

1. Mein Name 2. Ich 3. Ich 4. Mein Mann/Meine Frau

Accusative case

INTRODUCTION

Accusative describes the role of a particular noun or pronoun in a particular sentence.

EXPLANATION

Nouns and the words which accompany them (adjectives, **der/die/das** or **ein/kein/mein** etc.) or replace them (pronouns) are in the accusative case when they are the *direct object* of the verb, i.e. on the *receiving* end of the action.

Look at these examples:

Ich möchte *ein kaltes Bier*.	I'd like a cold beer.
***Den Mann* kann ich nicht leiden.**	I can't stand that man.
***Das* verstehe ich nicht.**	I don't understand that.
Rufen Sie *mich* bitte an.	Please give me a ring.
Kochen Sie *Kaffee*?	Are you making coffee?

All the *italicized* words are in the accusative case. In English the word order is quite rigid: 1. subject 2. verb 3. direct object; but as you can see, in German the accusative can be found almost anywhere in the sentence. This can be a bit confusing.

The clue is to look for the signs of the accusative:

1. Endings of **der/die/das, ein/kein/mein** etc.
2. Verb ending – tells you who is doing the action, and whether singular or plural. This helps you to narrow down the possibilities.
3. The meaning of the sentence as a whole – does it make sense?

HOW TO USE

If a noun is in the accusative case, you use the form you find in the dictionary for the singular or plural. The accompanying words look like this:

ACCUSATIVE ENDINGS

Singular			*Plural*
der group (**-n/-en** *ending*)	**die** group (**-e** *ending*)	**das** group (*no ending*)	all groups (**-e** *ending*)
den	**die**	**das**	**die**
einen	**eine**	**ein**	—
keinen	**keine**	**kein**	**keine**
meinen	**meine**	**mein**	**meine**
Ihren	**Ihre**	**Ihr**	**Ihre**

For the details about adjectives, see p.110.

As you can see, the accusative affects the **der** group much more than any other, and the sign to look for is the ending **-n**.

Pronouns in the accusative go like this:

Singular			*Plural*		
mich	(me)		**uns**	(us)	
ihn	(him/it)	to replace **den** words			
sie	(her/it)	to replace **die** words	**sie**	(them)	to replace **die** plural
es	(it)	to replace **das** words	**Sie**	(you)	
Sie	(you)				
sich	(yourself)		**sich**	(yourself)	

WHEN TO USE

1. With the direct object.

2. There are certain prepositions (see p.127) which always take the accusative case. The most common are: **für**, **durch** and **ohne**.

Das ist für *meinen* Sohn.	That's for my son.
Gehen Sie durch *den* Park.	Go through the park.

3. The prepositions **in/an/auf** with verbs of movement always take the accusative case.

Ich gehe heute abend *ins* Theater. (in das→ins)	I'm going to the theatre this evening.
Wir fahren morgen *in die* Stadt.	We're going into town tomorrow.
Gehen wir *an den* Strand?	Are we going to the beach?
Er fährt morgen *auf eine* Konferenz.	He's going to a conference tomorrow.

4. The expression **es gibt** (there is/there are) is always followed by the accusative case.

Es gibt *keinen* Aschenbecher.	There's no ashtray.
Gibt es hier in der Nähe *eine* Bank?	Is there a bank around here?

5. Expressions of time.

***einen* Moment**	just a moment
***diese* Woche**	this week
***nächstes* Jahr**	next year
Er war *eine* Woche krank.	He was ill for a week.
Ich bleibe *einen* Monat.	I'm staying for a month.

HOW TO USE

Once you have decided that a noun or pronoun is in the accusative case:

1. Decide whether your noun is singular or plural.
2. Decide which group it belongs to.
3. Choose the right ending for your accompanying word or replacement pronoun.

You want to say: 'I'd like an ice cream'. You know 'ice cream' is the direct object, therefore accusative case.

1. **Eis** is singular.
2. **Eis** belongs to the **das** group.
3. Therefore you say: **Ich möchte *ein Eis.***

You want to say: 'I'm looking for a present for my boyfriend'. You know 'present' is the direct object, therefore accusative case. 'My boyfriend' is accusative after **für** (see p.127).

1. Both **Geschenk** and **Freund** are singular.
2. **Geschenk** belongs to the **das** group, **Freund** to the **der** group.
3. Therefore you say: **Ich suche *ein Geschenk* für *meinen Freund.***

Now go back and look at all the examples once again to make sure you understand.

Here are some important phrases for when you stay in a German hotel. Look at the English translation then fill in the correct form of the missing words. They are all accusative.

1. **Haben Sie … Zimmer frei?**	Have you got a room?
2. **Ich möchte … Doppelzimmer für zwei …**	I'd like a double room for two nights.
3. **Kann ich hier … Reisescheck einlösen?**	Can I cash a traveller's check here?
4. **Können Sie bitte … Hundertmarkschein wechseln?**	Can you please change a 100 Mark note?
5. **Gibt es hier … Telefon?**	Is there a telephone here?
6. **Gibt es hier … Toilette?**	Is there a toilet here?
7. **Gibt es hier … Reinigung?**	Is there a cleaning service here?
8. **Gibt es hier … Parkplatz?**	Is there a car park here?
9. **Ich verstehe … nicht.**	I don't understand you.
10. **Gibt es Post für …?**	Is there any post for me?
11. **Das ist für …**	That's for you.
12. **Könnten Sie … bitte um 8 Uhr wecken?**	Could you please give me a call at 8 o'clock?
13. **Ich möchte … Zeitung.**	I'd like a newspaper.
14. **Ich möchte … Kännchen Kaffee.**	I'd like a pot of coffee.
15. **Ich möchte … Aschenbecher.**	I'd like an ashtray.
16. **… Augenblick bitte.**	Just a minute please.
17. **Ich hole … Gepäck.**	I'll get my luggage.
18. **Ich hole … Koffer.**	I'll get my suitcase.
19. **Ich hole … Tasche.**	I'll get my bag.
20. **Ich hole … Auto.**	I'll get my car.

ANSWERS

1. ein 2. ein, Nächte 3. einen 4. einen 5. ein 6. eine 7. eine 8. einen 9. Sie 10. mich 11. Sie 12. mich 13. eine 14. ein 15. einen 16. einen 17. mein 18. meinen 19. meine 20. mein

Dative case

INTRODUCTION

Although we virtually possess no dative case in English it is extremely important in German, particularly in many common phrases which occur in personal conversations such as enquiring after someone's well-being, whether they are enjoying their meal, what they like and dislike etc.

EXPLANATION

Nouns and the words which accompany them (**der/die/das, ein/kein/mein** etc., adjectives) or replace them (pronouns) are in the dative case when they are the *indirect object* of the verb. In English we tend to use 'to'/'for' to indicate the indirect object, but the Germans prefer to use endings to signpost the dative.

First let us be quite sure what we mean by indirect object. If we take a sentence like 'I bought myself a lovely coat yesterday', we can break down the sentence as follows:

Subject of verb	= I
Verb	= bought
Object of verb	= a lovely coat

But what about 'myself'? I didn't hand over money and buy myself. I bought a lovely coat *for* myself. This is what we mean by the indirect object as distinct from the direct object – 'a lovely coat'.

Here are some more examples. The dative is italicized.

Zeigen Sie *mir* bitte auf der Karte.	Please show *me* on the map (show to me).
Er hat *uns* die Zeitung gebracht.	He brought *us* the newspaper (i.e. brought to us).

The most common verbs you will find with an indirect object are: **geben** (to give), **bringen** (to bring), **zeigen** (to show), **kaufen** (to buy), **schicken** (to send), **sagen** (to say, tell).

HOW TO USE

How do you recognise the dative in German? The word order in the sentence won't help you very much, so you will have to recognise the endings which signpost the dative, which are:

for **der/das** group words	**-m**	(think of him)
for **die** group words	**-r**	(think of her)
for all plural words	**-n**	

Look at the patterns:

DATIVE ENDINGS

Singular			*Plural*
der group (**-m** ending)	**die** group (**-r** ending)	**das** group (**-m** ending)	all groups (**-n** ending) + noun adds **-n/-en**
dem	**der**	**dem**	**den**
einem	**einer**	**einem**	—
keinem	**keiner**	**keinem**	**keinen**
meinem	**meiner**	**meinem**	**meinen**
Ihrem	**Ihrer**	**Ihrem**	**Ihren**

The pronouns in the dative go:

Singular		*Plural*	
mir (me)		**uns** (us)	
ihm (him/it)	to replace **dem** words		
ihr (her/it)	to replace **der** words	**ihnen** (them)	to replace **den** plural
ihm (it)	to replace **dem** words		
Ihnen (you)		**Ihnen** (you)	
sich (yourself)		**sich** (yourself)	

As you can see, every group is affected by the dative so try to learn the signposts above. Does it matter? Yes and no. You can get away with swallowing in the right places and bluffing. I suggest you at least try to remember **mir** and **Ihnen** because they occur very frequently and are much more noticeable than the others if you get them wrong. For those who would like to sound correct try learning our examples by heart, but don't get too preoccupied with being correct – it takes the Germans years to learn it at school!

EXPLANATION

1. The dative case is also used with other types of phrases which mean 'to like something' 'to belong' (to).

Es gefällt *mir*.	I like it (people, things, places).
Es schmeckt *mir*.	I like it (food, drink). Literally: 'it tastes good to me'.
Schmeckt *Ihnen* der Wein?	Do you like the wine?
Das gehört *mir*.	That belongs to me.

2. Some very common expressions which must be learned by heart:

Guten Tag, wie geht es *Ihnen*?	Hallo, how are you?
Danke, es geht *mir* gut.	I'm very well thank you.
Und wie geht es *Ihrem Mann/ Ihrer Frau*?	And how's your husband/wife?
***Mir* ist schlecht.**	I'm not feeling very well.
Oh, das tut *mir* leid.	Oh, I'm sorry.
Ist *Ihnen* zu warm/kalt?	Are you too hot/cold?
***Mir* ist warm/kalt.**	I'm too hot/cold.
Das ist *mir* egal.	I don't care.

3. With a few verbs which in English do not take an indirect object: **helfen** (to help), **danken** (to thank), **glauben** (to believe).

Wir glauben *ihm* nicht.	We don't believe him.
Kann ich Ihnen helfen?	Can I help you?
Ich danke *Ihnen*.	Thank you.

4. When describing some personal activities where in English we would use 'my/your/his' etc.

Ich will *mir* die Zähne putzen.	I want to clean my teeth.
Ich lasse *mir* die Haare schneiden.	I'm going to have my hair cut.

5. After many prepositions (see p.127). The commonest are **bei**, **zu**, **mit**, **von**, **nach**.

Wir haben *mit den Kindern* gespielt.	We played with the children.
Ich wohne *bei meinen Eltern*.	I live with my parents.
***Nach den* neuesten Nachrichten.**	According to the latest news.

6. After the prepositions **an/in/auf** with a verb describing position (see p. 127).

Ich wohne *in der* Dahlemstraße.	I live in Dahlemstraße.
Die Zeitung liegt *auf dem* Tisch.	The newspaper is on the table.

HOW TO USE

Having decided that the word you want to use is dative,

1. Decide whether your noun is singular or plural.
2. Decide which group it belongs to (**der/die/das**).
3. Choose the right ending for your accompanying word or replacement pronoun.

You want to say: 'Give him the book'.

1. 'Him' is singular.
2. 'Him' is a pronoun replacing a **dem** word.
3. Therefore you say: **Geben Sie *ihm* das Buch.**

You want to say: 'How's your brother today?'

1. **Bruder** is singular.
2. **Bruder** is a **der** group word.
3. Therefore you say: **Wie geht es *Ihrem Bruder*?**

PRACTICE/LEARN BY HEART

Here are some very useful phrases for personal conversations. Try to fill in the blanks. They are all dative and are in our examples above.

1. **Kann ich … helfen?**	Can I help you?
2. **… ist schlecht.**	I feel sick.
3. **Wie geht es …?**	How are you?
4. **Wie geht es … Frau?**	How's your wife?
5. **Die Bluse gefällt …**	I like the blouse.
6. **Schmeckt … der Wein?**	Do you like the wine?
7. **Oh, das tut … leid.**	Oh, I am sorry.

ANSWERS

1. Ihnen 2. Mir 3. Ihnen 4. Ihrer 5. mir 6. Ihnen 7. mir

Genitive case

INTRODUCTION
Genitive means possessive, and the genitive case is a way of showing who owns what. It translates English 's or 'of', e.g. 'My brother's car', 'the top of the hill' etc.

HOW TO USE
This is what the genitive looks like:

der group	die group	das group	plural
des + -s or -es on noun eines + -(e)s keines + -(e)s meines + -(e)s	der einer keiner meiner	des + -s or -es on noun eines + -(e)s keines + -(e)s meines + -(e)s	der — keiner meiner

Notice that for **der/das** group words **-s** or **-es** is added on to the noun. For **die** group and plural words there is no extra ending for the noun.

In addition to showing possession the genitive case is also used after some prepositions and other expressions: **während** (during); **wegen** (because of); **trotz** (in spite of); **aufgrund** (because of); **im Laufe** (in the course of/during); **in der Nähe** (near).

Examples:

Ist das das Haus Ihr*er* Eltern?	Is this your parents' house?
Das ist Onkel Fritz, der Bruder mein*er* Mutter.	This is uncle Fritz, my mother's brother.
Das können wir während *des Essens* besprechen.	We can talk about that over lunch.
Wir hören im Laufe *des Tages* von ihm.	We'll hear from him in the course of the day.
Das ist der Wagen *meines* Freund*es*.	This is my friend's car.
Man sieht den Gipfel *des* Berg*es* nicht.	You can't see the summit of the mountain.
Angebot *des* Monat*s*	Special offer of the month
Auto *des* Jahr*es*	Car of the year

With people's names you add **s**:
Petras Bruder **Hermanns Schwester** etc.

To sum up: the sign of the genitive for **der/das** words is **-s** + **-s** or **-es** ending on the noun, and for **die** words and plural it is **-r** + no special ending for the noun.

The definite article

INTRODUCTION

'The' is a relatively minor piece of English grammar because it has only one form, but in German the words for 'the' are extremely important. There are several forms for the word 'the'. Every noun (see p.75) belongs to one of three groups. If you look up a noun in a dictionary, you will probably find something like: n.m. (noun, masculine) or n.f. (noun, feminine) or n.n. (noun, neuter) after it to tell you which group it belongs to.

der group (n.m. in dictionary)
die group (n.f. in dictionary)
das group (n.n. in dictionary)

Der/die/das etc. are used whenever we use 'the' in English, and they nearly always are followed by a noun. Before you decide which form of **der/die/das** to use you have to know a few things about the accompanying noun:

1. whether it is singular or plural;
2. which **der/die/das** group it belongs to;
3. what role it plays in this particular sentence (i.e. case, see p.80).

EXPLANATION

Look at the pattern:

	Singular			*Plural for all 3 groups*
	der group	**die** group	**das** group	
Nom.	**der**	**die**	**das**	**die**
Acc.	**den**	**die**	**das**	**die**
Dat.	**dem**	**der**	**dem**	**den**
Gen.	**des**	**der**	**des**	**der**

This looks a bit much but you will help yourself to learn the important bits if you concentrate on two ideas:

1. Reduce your learning to the minimum by remembering: nominative and accusative are the same for all groups except the **der** (masculine singular) group, in which **der** changes to **den** in the accusative.

And for the dative remember:

-m ending for **der/das** groups
-r ending for **die** group
-n ending for all plurals

2. These endings set the pattern for many other endings. If you learn them thoroughly now, you will find other grammar points much easier to cope with.

HOW TO USE

In order to decide which form of **der/die/das** is the correct one, you have to follow three steps:

1. Decide whether the accompanying noun is singular or plural;
2. If it is singular, which group does it belong to?
3. What role does it play in this sentence? (which case?)

For example, you wish to say: 'The car is in the garage'.

1. Both nouns are singular.
2. **Das Auto; die Garage.**
3. **Auto** is nominative because it is the subject of the verb. **Garage** is dative after **in** + dative for position (see p.128).

Das Auto ist in der Garage.

You wish to ask: 'Where are the toilets?'

1. 'Toilets' is a plural noun.
2. Does not apply here.
3. **Toiletten** is nominative because it is the subject of the verb.

Wo sind die Toiletten?

WHEN TO USE

Der/die/das is used just the same as 'the' in English, for example:

Wo ist das Telefon?	Where's the telephone?
Wo ist die Tür?	Where is the door?
Wann kommt der nächste Bus?	When's the next bus?

Der/die/das is sometimes used differently from English 'the':

1. With people's names. You will often hear German people refer to friends and relatives as: **der Peter, die Monika, der Schmidt** etc. This is colloquial and only acceptable when you are on very friendly terms.

2. **Die meisten** = most

Die meisten Engländer trinken Tee mit Milch.	Most English people drink tea with milk.

3. With prices, **der/die/das** = per

Zwanzig Pfennig das Stück.	Twenty Pfennigs per piece.
Zehn Mark das Kilo.	Ten Marks per kilo.

4. The names of some countries:

die Schweiz	Switzerland
die BRD (die Bundesrepublik Deutschland)	The Federal Republic of Germany
die DDR (die Deutsche Demokratische Republik)	The German Democratic Republic
die Sowjetunion	The Soviet Union
die USA/die Vereinigten Staaten	The USA/The United States
die Türkei	Turkey
die Niederlande	The Netherlands

LEARN BY HEART

Nobody expects you to know the **der/die/das** group for every noun in the German language but you will help yourself a great deal if you try to learn the common ones at least.

Here are some places you will find at any German station or airport. It will help you to be able to ask where to find them:

1. **Entschuldigen Sie bitte, wo ist ... Restaurant?**	Excuse me, where is the restaurant?
2. **Entschuldigen Sie bitte, wo ist ... Auskunft?**	Excuse me, where is the information desk?
3. **Entschuldigen Sie bitte, wo ist ... Taxistand?**	Excuse me, where is the taxi stand?
4. **Entschuldigen Sie bitte, wo ist ... Wechselstube?**	Excuse me, where is the exchange kiosk?
5. **Entschuldigen Sie bitte, wo sind ... Toiletten?**	Excuse me, where are the toilets?

ANSWERS

1. das 2. die 3. der 4. die 5. die

The indefinite article

INTRODUCTION

The indefinite article ('a', 'an') is used when you are not referring to any specific object already mentioned. In German, you use the word **ein** or one of its forms. **Ein** always accompanies a noun, and therefore it has endings which change depending on the **der/die/das** group the noun belongs to and also the role the noun is playing in that particular sentence (i.e. case). 'A'/'an' is a very straightforward little word in English, but in German **ein** has a whole system of endings.

EXPLANATION

Look at these examples:

Ich möchte *eine* Tasse Kaffee.	I'd like *a* cup of coffee.
Haben Sie *einen* Bleistift?	Have you got *a* pencil?
Gibt es hier in der Nähe *eine* Bushaltestelle?	Is there *a* bus stop near here?

Warning! If you have a negative sentence involving 'not a'/'not an', you must on no account say **nicht ein**. Instead you must always use **kein** or one of its forms. This is a very important German grammar point (see p.70).

HOW TO USE

	der group	die group	das group
Nom.	**ein**	**eine**	**ein**
Acc.	**einen**	**eine**	**ein**
Dat.	**einem**	**einer**	**einem**
Gen.	**eines**	**einer**	**eines**

This pattern is important because it is the model for **kein** and the possessive adjectives (**mein**, **ihr** etc.) (see p.120; see also p.161 for the overall picture of endings).

Checklist for using **ein**:

1. Decide which group the accompanying noun belongs to (**der/die/das**).
2. Decide which role the noun is playing in the particular sentence.

You want to say: 'I have a son and a daughter'.
1. **Der Sohn, die Tochter.**
2. Both nouns are accusative because they are the object of the verb.
So you say: **Ich habe *einen* Sohn und *eine* Tochter.**

You want to say: 'I am staying with a family in Berlin'.
1. **Die Familie**
2. 'Family' is dative after **bei** (see p.131).
So you say: **Ich wohne bei *einer* Familie in Berlin.**

PRACTICE/LEARN BY HEART

Using the checklist above, fill in the correct form of **ein**:

1. **Was kostet ein– Kilo?**	How much is a kilo?
2. **Das ist ein– schöne Wohnung.**	This is a lovely flat.
3. **Haben Sie ein– Zimmmer frei?**	Have you got a room?
4. **Ich möchte ein– Schachtel Zigaretten.**	I'd like a packet of cigarettes.
5. **Wir haben ein– guten Film gesehen.**	We saw a good film.

WHEN TO USE

There are a few situations when English 'a/an' is different from German:

1. With people's jobs, miss out **ein** in German:

Sie ist Sekretärin.	She's *a* secretary.
Ich bin Ingenieur.	I'm *an* engineer.

2. In expressions of time, use **pro** (=per)

einmal *pro* Woche	once *a* week
zweimal *pro* Tag	twice *a* day

3. Expressions like 'half a', 'such a', 'what a':

***ein halbes* Pfund Edamer**	half *a* pound of Edam
***So ein* netter Junge!**	what *a* nice boy!
***so eine* nette Überraschung!**	what *a* nice surprise!

4. 'A lot of' = **viel**

Er hat viel Geld.	He has a lot of money.

ANSWERS
1. ein 2. eine 3. ein 4. eine 5. einen

Pronouns

INTRODUCTION

Pronouns make our language neater and more compact. Onçe we have mentioned 'the lady who lives down the road with her husband and ten cats', we don't want to repeat all this each time we talk about the lady, so we use *she* and *her* to replace the long description. In other words, once we have established who or what we are talking about, we use pronouns as a quick reference.

EXPLANATION

Pronouns refer to people and things and they often replace nouns. Therefore they also have cases, depending on their function in the sentence. If you are not quite sure what cases are, look up p.80. The endings of verbs also change depending on the noun or pronoun doing the action.

Personal pronouns

1. Refer to people:

Nom. *Acc.* *Dat.*	**ich** (I) **mich** (me) **mir** (me)	**Sie** (you) **Sie** (you) **Ihnen** (you)	**wir** (we) **uns** (us) **uns** (us)

2. Refer to people and things and replace nouns:

Replace	**der** group	**die** group	**das** group	*Plural* all groups
Nom. *Acc.* *Dat.*	**er** (he/it) **ihn** (him/it) **ihm** (him/it)	**sie** (she/it) **sie** (her/it) **ihr** (her/it)	**es** (it) **es** (it) **ihm** (it)	**sie** (they) **sie** (them) **ihnen** (them)

It looks a lot, but can you see any patterns to help you? Look at p.161 for an overall picture of patterns.

Notes

1. **Sie** is the polite form of *you*. Always use it unless you are on extremely friendly terms. For the informal **du** etc. see p.103. As in English, **Sie** is both singular and plural. The verb always ends in **-en**. **Sie** and **Ihnen** (meaning 'you') are always written with a capital letter.

Sometimes it's difficult to work out in a conversation whether **Sie/sie** means *you/she/it/they*. Then it's important to listen for the verb ending. If it's **-t**, **Sie/sie** means *she* or *it* and you have to recall whether a thing or a person (female) has been mentioned. If it's **-en**, **sie** means *you* or *they/them*. If it's *they/them*, there must have been a noun somewhere along the line. If you've lost track, ask **wer?** (who?) or **was?** (what?).

2. **It** in English always refers to things. But in German, things belong to all three groups of nouns (**der/die/das**). So if you were talking about a thing in the **der** group you would replace it by **er/ihn/ihm** depending on the case.

Wo ist der Tisch? Ich sehe *ihn* nicht.

Wo ist meine Bluse? Ich finde *sie* nicht.

So don't be tempted to say **es** for *it* every time. It's just as likely to be a variation of **er** or **sie**.

3. Notice that **ich** (I) is written with a small letter when not the first word in a sentence.

HOW TO USE

When using pronouns, follow these three steps:

1. Decide whether the noun or pronoun is singular or plural.
2. Decide which group it belongs to: **der – er, die – sie, das – es.**
3. Decide which case it is in.

You want to say: '*He* (my brother) is very happy there'.

1. *He* is singular.
2. *He* is replacing a **der** group word, **Bruder**, brother.
3. *He* is nominative, because subject of *is*.

So you say: ***Er* ist sehr glücklich dort.**

You want to say: 'Could you help us please?'

1. *You* could be singular or plural, *us* is plural.
2. *You* and *us* are not replacing nouns.
3. *You* is nominative (doing the action), *us* is dative after **helfen**.

So you say: **Könnten *Sie uns* bitte helfen?**

PRACTICE

Now try this exercise. Fill in the blanks and replace the italicized phrases with pronouns.

1. **... bin mit *der Kamera* sehr zufrieden.**	I'm very pleased with the camera.
2. **... fahre mit *meinem Freund* in die Stadt.**	I'm going into town with my friend.
3. ***Mein Bruder* hat den *roten Wagen* gekauft.**	My brother bought the red car.
4. ***Die Leute* sind von überallher.**	The people have come from all over the place.
5. **... können *das Zelt* da drüben aufstellen.**	We can put the tent up over there.

LEARN BY HEART

Here are some useful expressions with personal pronouns to express how people feel, what they want etc.

***Ich* habe Hunger/Durst.**	I'm hungry/thirsty.
***Mir* ist kalt/warm.**	I'm cold/hot.
***Wir* frieren/schwitzen.**	We're freezing/boiling hot.
***Ich* muß auf die Toilette.**	I have to go to the toilet.
Es tut *mir* weh.	It hurts.
***Ich* habe Kopfschmerzen.**	I've got a headache.
***Ihm/ihr* ist schlecht.**	He/she is feeling sick.
***Er* ist ganz blaß.**	He's very pale.
Es geht *ihm/ihr* gut.	He/she's fine.
Sind *Sie* müde/krank/nervös?	Are you tired/ill/nervous?
Haben *Sie* Schmerzen?	Are you in pain?
Wie geht es *Ihnen*?	How are you?

ANSWERS

1. Ich, ihr 2. Ich, ihm 3. Er, ihn 4. Sie 5. Wir, es

man

INTRODUCTION

man is an impersonal pronoun. You will come across it particularly when reading or being given instructions, asking for suggestions or help, talking about official regulations or making very general statements or questions.

EXPLANATION

man is a very useful little word. It can be used to translate the English words: one, people, someone, you (impersonal), they (not specific). It also offers a convenient way of avoiding the passive (see p.47) in German. It can be used whenever you don't want to be specific about a person or people.

Look at these examples:

Man trinkt viel Tee in England.	They drink a lot of tea in England.
Hier muß man immer lange warten.	You always have to wait a long time here.
Hier kann man überall gut essen.	You can get a good meal everywhere here.
Man spricht Englisch.	English spoken (sign in shop).
Hier darf man nicht rauchen.	Smoking not permitted.
Wie sagt man das auf deutsch?	What's the German for that? (*Lit.* How do you say it in German?)
Man hat mir gesagt ...	I was told .../Someone said to me ...

HOW TO USE

man is a pronoun and therefore it has cases:

Nom.	**man**
Acc.	**einen**
Dat.	**einem**

In practice, you will probably only need to use **man**. **Man** takes the same verb ending as **er/sie/es** which is **-t**.

Man verdien*t* gut hier.	The pay is good here. (One earns well here.)

Warning: Don't get **man** (one/you/people etc.) mixed up with **Mann** (husband/man).

LEARN BY HEART

Here are some questions you might want to use:

1. **Wo wirft man das Geld ein?**	Where do you (does one) insert the money?
2. **Wo kann man Geld wechseln?**	Where can you (can one) change money?
3. **Was kann man da machen?**	What is there to do there?
4. **Was kann man in der Stadt unternehmen?**	What is there to do in the town?
5. **Wie kommt man am besten dahin?**	What's the best way to get there?
6. **Wie kommt man am besten zur Autobahn?**	What's the best way to get to the motorway?
7. **Wie spricht man das aus?**	How do you (does one) pronounce that?
8. **Kann man das reparieren?**	Can it be repaired?
9. **Braucht man ein Visum/eine Karte?**	Do you (does one) need a visa/ticket?

du / ihr

INTRODUCTION

One of the most important things about learning a foreign language is to develop an awareness of when certain words are appropriate – and when they are not. This is as important to good communication as vocabulary and grammar. English-speaking people in particular should be careful when they use the familiar forms **du** ('you', singular) and **ihr** ('you', plural) – using them at the wrong time could create dreadful misunderstandings, even lose you a business contract or land you in a stand-up fight.

WHEN TO USE

It is perfectly OK to use **du/ihr** when talking to children or animals. However, do not use **du/ihr** with adults:

1. If you are a child/teenager/student etc. and they are vastly your senior – even if they call you **du**.

2. Unless you are a member of a group of e.g. students, fellow golfers etc. who are all pals together, and everybody uses **du** to each other.

3. Unless your German friend/business contact etc. suggests you both call each other **du**. This will quite often be accompanied by a formal drinking to the new intimate relationship. The suggestion might be made like this:

Wollen wir uns nicht duzen?	Shall we call each other *du*?

Duzen means 'to say **du** to someone', or to be on first-name terms.

The reason that **du/ihr** present problems for English speakers is that in English we have only one word 'you' to cover all degrees of formality. We express formality or informality, keep our distance or get friendly quickly by using titles and names in different ways. Have you ever felt slightly affronted when someone has called you by your first name and you weren't quite ready to get on such friendly terms? Something similar happens if you use **du** to a German acquaintance. They will probably feel a bit insulted, and certainly embarrassed.

With **du** you use first names. Once you are on **du** terms with somebody you have established a familiar relationship. It is virtually impossible to go back on the decision to say **du** to someone, even if you decide that you don't like them very much after all or don't want to be on such familiar terms. That is why the Germans are a bit wary at first of offering **du** to new acquaintances. It does not mean that they are being unfriendly.

Therefore, for most people most of the time, the safest thing is always to use **Sie + Herr/Frau/Fräulein +** surname to all adults unless any of the conditions 1–3 above apply.

HOW TO USE

1. Verbs.

The **du** form of the verb ends in **-st**, the **ihr** form ends in **-t**.

Present tense

For weak verbs add **-st**	add **-t**
du machst, du frühstückst etc.	**ihr macht, ihr frühstückt**

For strong verbs there is often a stem change in the **du** form, but not in the **ihr** form.

schlafen	**du schläfst**	**ihr schlaft**
lesen	**du liest**	**ihr lest**
nehmen	**du nimmst**	**ihr nehmt**

For modal verbs add **-st** to the **ich/er/sie/es** form to make the **du** form, add **-t** to the infinitive stem to make the **ihr** form.

wollen	**du willst**	**ihr wollt**
können	**du kannst**	**ihr könnt**

Imperative
For the **du** imperative take off the **-st** ending from the **du** form of the present tense. Strong verbs which take an Umlaut in the present tense lose it in the imperative. The **ihr** imperative is the same as the **ihr** form of the present tense.

schlafen	**schlaf**	**schlaft**
nehmen	**nimm**	**nehmt**

Schlaf gut!	Sleep well!
Sei still!	Keep still!
Komm her!	Come here!

Imperfect tense
For the **du** form, add **-st** and for the **ihr** form, add **-t** to the usual imperfect stem.

Weak verbs:
du machtest, du fragtest etc. — **ihr machtet, ihr fragtet** etc.

Strong verbs:
du aßt (from **essen**), **du nahmst** (from **nehmen**) etc. — **ihr aßt, ihr nahmt** etc.

Modal verbs:
du mußtest (from **müssen**), **du wolltest** (from **wollen**) etc. — **ihr mußtet, ihr wolltet** etc.

Perfect tense
Use **du hast/ihr habt; du bist/ihr seid.** } + past participle in the usual way (see p.18)

Pluperfect tense
Use **du hattest, du warst/ihr hattet, ihr wart** + past participle in the usual way (see p.24).

Future
Use **du wirst/ihr werdet** + infinitive (see p.25).

Passive
Use **du wirst/ihr werdet** + past participle for the present tense. Use **du wurdest/ihr wurdet** + past participle for the imperfect tense (see p.47).

2. Personal pronouns

Nom.	**du**	**ihr**
Acc.	**dich**	**euch**
Dat.	**dir**	**euch**

N.B. in letter writing, **du** and **ihr** are written with a capital letter.

Here are some examples of **du/ihr** to give you a feeling for how to use them.

Hast du die Tür zugemacht?	Have you shut the door?
Kannst du dich erinnern?	Can you remember?
Mach dir keine Sorgen.	Don't worry.
Ich gebe dir den Schlüssel.	I'll give you the key.
Wolltest du auch mitfahren?	Did you want to go too?
Setz dich.	Sit down.
Was wollt ihr jetzt machen?	What do you want to do now?
Was habt ihr vor?	What are you intending to do?
Können wir heute zu euch kommen?	Can we come to your place today?
Wie geht es euch?	How are you?
Wie gefällt euch die Wohnung?	How do you like the flat?
Bitte setzt euch.	Please sit down.
Bitte kommt herein.	Please come in.

3. Possessive adjectives

dein **euer**

They follow the same pattern of endings as **ein/mein** etc. (see p.97).

Relative pronouns

INTRODUCTION

We use relative pronouns ('who', 'which' etc.) to refer to specific people or things we have already mentioned in a previous part of the sentence. In English, we use 'who' (or 'whom') for people and 'which' or 'that' for things. Sometimes we omit the relative pronoun altogether, but nevertheless it is still understood to be there. Look at these examples: 'This is the girl *who* helped me'; 'Have you got any pills *which* are effective against migraine?'; 'The man I want to see is away today' (*whom* is omitted); 'That's the drink I tried yesterday' (*which* is omitted).

EXPLANATION

Relative pronouns act as a bridge between one clause and another. They refer back to an object or person in the previous clause and they also play an important grammatical role in their own clause.

In German the relative pronouns are:

	for **der** words	for **die** words	for **das** words	for plural words
Nom.	**der**	**die**	**das**	**die**
Acc.	**den**	**die**	**das**	**die**
Dat.	**dem**	**der**	**dem**	**denen**
Gen.	**dessen**	**deren**	**dessen**	**deren**

As you can see there is a very close connection between the relative pronoun and the **der/die/das** form of the word it refers to. There is no separate form for 'who' and 'which'.

HOW TO USE

Like all pronouns, relative pronouns have different endings depending on:
1. whether the noun they refer back to is singular or plural;
2. which **der/die/das** group it belongs to;
3. which role the relative pronoun is playing in its own clause (i.e. case).

Examples:

Der Film, *der* heute im Fernsehen läuft, ist sehr gut. The film *which* is on TV today is very good.
1. **Film** is singular.
2. **Film** is a **der** word.
3. 'Which' is nominative in its part of the sentence because it is the subject of **läuft**.

Der Wagen, *den* ich gemietet habe, ist kaputt. The car I have rented has broken down.
1. **Wagen** is singular.
2. **Wagen** is a **der** word.
3. 'Which' (understood) is accusative in its part of the sentence because it is the object of **ich habe gemietet**.

You can also use relative pronouns with prepositions ('with', 'from' etc.).

Das ist die Frau, von *der* ich die Tasche gekauft habe.	That's the lady I bought the bag from (from *whom* I bought the bag).

1. **Frau** is singular.
2. **Frau** is a **die** word.
3. 'Whom' (understood) is dative after **von**.

Das sind die Leute, mit *denen* ich zusammen arbeite.	Those are the people I work with (with *whom* I work).

1. **Leute** is plural.
2. Not relevant because **Leute** is plural.
3. 'Whom' (understood) is dative after **mit**.

You probably think of **der/die/das** only as meaning 'the', so this role as 'who'/'which' takes a bit of getting used to. Study the examples carefully to make sure you follow what is going on.

Notes:
1. Notice the comma which comes before the relative pronoun. It looks strange to us but is absolutely essential in German because it marks the boundaries of the clauses. You don't take a breath or make any pause to interrupt the flow of the sentence when you are speaking.
2. You *never* leave out the relative pronoun in German.
3. The relative pronoun sends the verb in its clause to the end. Here are some more examples:

Wie heißt der Mann, *der* gegenüber von uns wohnt?	What's the name of the man who lives opposite us?
Haben Sie noch das Kleid, *das* ich gestern anprobiert habe?	Have you still got the dress I tried on yesterday?

LEARN BY HEART

Fill in the correct relative pronoun.

1. **Das ist die Stadt, in ... ich gewohnt habe.**	That's the town where (in which) I lived.
2. **Ist das der Mantel, ... Sie suchen?**	Is this the coat (which) you are looking for?

3. **Ist das der Brief, ... gestern gekommen ist?**	Is that the letter which arrived yesterday?
4. **Das sind die Leute, mit ... ich nach Paris gefahren bin.**	Those are the people I went to Paris with (with whom).
5. **Kennen Sie den Mann, mit ... ich gesprochen habe?**	Do you know the man I spoke to (with whom I spoke)?

ANSWERS

1. der 2. den 3. der 4. denen 5. dem

Adjectives

INTRODUCTION

Adjectives describe nouns. They make our language more picturesque, they fill out bald statements consisting of nouns and verbs:
The cat sat on the mat.
The *large*, *fluffy*, *Persian* cat sat on the *beautiful red* and *green* mat.
I want a coat.
I want a *short*, *navy blue* coat with *red* trimmings. Not too *expensive* but *smart* and *attractive*.

You can't learn German adjectives in a day – so don't try! But don't give up either. Persevere, and one day you will be able to use German adjectives with confidence (and correctly, 90% of the time – which is better than many German native speakers).

HOW TO USE

Because adjectives accompany nouns, they are directly affected by:
1. whether the noun is singular or plural;
2. which **der/die/das** group the noun belongs to;
3. what case the noun is in;
4. whether the noun is accompanied by **der/die/das** or **ein/kein/mein** or nothing at all.

Basically there are four different situations affecting adjective endings. This sounds rather a lot to take in, but it does have a certain logic and the important thing is to try and group the basic patterns.

Situation Type One

Adjective standing on its own, without a noun or after the verb **sein** (to be) or **werden** (to become):

schön!	lovely!
toll!	great!
Das ist schön!	That's lovely!
Die Bluse ist schön.	The blouse is beautiful.
Das Wetter wird schön.	The weather's getting nice.
Die Kleider sind schön.	The dresses are beautiful.

You use the adjective just as it appears in the dictionary, without any endings.

Situation Type Two

Der/die/das + adjective + noun:

	der group	die group	das group
Nom.	**der rot*e* Pullover**	**die grün*e* Bluse**	**das blau*e* Kleid**
Acc.	**den rot*en* Pullover**	**die grün*e* Bluse**	**das blau*e* Kleid**
Dat.	**dem rot*en* Pullover**	**der grün*en* Bluse**	**dem blau*en* Kleid**
Gen.	**des rot*en* Pullovers**	**der grün*en* Bluse**	**des blau*en* Kleides**

	Plural
Nom.	**die weiß*en* Schuhe**
Acc.	**die weiß*en* Schuhe**
Dat.	**den weiß*en* Schuhen**
Gen.	**der weiß*en* Schuhe**

Here are some common phrases with the accusative in this situation. They are all expressions of time:

Ich war *die ganze Woche* krank.	I was ill all week.
Er wartet schon den ganzen Tag.	He's been waiting all day.
Das Hotel ist *das ganze Jahr* geöffnet.	The hotel is open all year.

The dative is often used to describe where things are, so here are some common examples in this situation:

Auf der rechten Seite	On the right hand side
Im zweiten Stock	On the second floor.
In der ersten Etage	On the first floor.
Im blauen Koffer	In the blue case.
In der großen Halle	In the main hall.

Situation Type Three

Ein/kein/mein/Ihr + adjective + noun:

	der group	die group	das group
Nom.	**ein gut*er* Rotwein**	**eine warm*e* Mahlzeit**	**ein kalt*es* Bier**
Acc.	**einen gut*en* Rotwein**	**eine warm*e* Mahlzeit**	**ein kalt*es* Bier**
Dat.	**einem gut*en* Rotwein**	**einer warm*en* Mahlzeit**	**einem kalt*en* Bier**
Gen.	**eines gut*en* Rotweins**	**einer warm*en* Mahlzeit**	**eines kalt*en* Biers**

	Plural
Nom.	**keine neu*en* Kartoffeln**
Acc.	**keine neu*en* Kartoffeln**
Dat.	**keinen neu*en* Kartoffeln**
Gen.	**keiner neu*en* Kartoffeln**

Try to learn the rhythm of these groups and concentrate on learning the nominative and accusative forms. If you can remember **ein guter Wein** (**der** words) and **ein kaltes Bier** (**das** words), you are well on your way to sorting them out. Nearly all the others take **-n**.

Situation Type Four

Adjective + noun, no **der/die/das** or **ein/kein/mein/Ihr**. Here the adjective takes on the endings which you would normally put on **der/die/das** except in the genitive. The adjective has to take on this job because otherwise you wouldn't know what role the noun was playing in the sentence.

	der words	die words	das words
Nom.	**gut*er* Wein**	**schön*e* Landschaft**	**deutsch*es* Geld**
Acc.	**gut*en* Wein**	**schön*e* Landschaft**	**deutsch*es* Geld**
Dat.	**gut*em* Wein**	**schön*er* Landschaft**	**deutsch*em* Geld**
Gen.	**gut*en* Weins**	**schön*er* Landschaft**	**deutsch*en* Geldes**

	Plural
Nom.	**nette Leute**
Acc.	**nette Leute**
Dat.	**netten Leuten**
Gen.	**netter Leute**

Here are some examples of this use of adjectives that you would find on labels:

reine Baumwolle	pure cotton
In brochures:	
ruhige Lage	quiet situation
fließendes Wasser	running water
At the market:	
frische Eier	fresh eggs
And talking to people:	
Guten Tag	Hello
Guten Abend	Good evening
Gute Fahrt	Have a good trip
Gute Reise	Have a good journey
Guten Appetit	Enjoy your meal
Gute Besserung	Get well soon

This is the sort of thought process you have to go through when using adjectives: You want to say: 'I haven't any German money.'
Geld is
1. singular;
2. a **das** word;
3. accusative;
4. the situation is type three.

So you say: **Ich habe kei*n* deutsch*es* Geld.**

You want to say: 'Where are my black shoes?'
Schuhe is
1. plural;
2. **der/die/das** group not relevant;
3. nominative;
4. the situation is type three.

So you say: **Wo sind mein*e* schwarz*en* Schuhe?**

You want to say: 'I'd like a good red wine'.
Rotwein is
1. singular;
2. a **der** word;
3. accusative;
4. the situation is type three.

So you say: **Ich möchte ein*en* gut*en* Rotwein.**

You want to say: 'Do you know the old man over there?'
Mann is
1. singular;
2. a **der** word;
3. accusative;
4. the situation is type two.

So you say: **Kennen Sie d*en* alt*en* Mann da drüben?**

You want to say: 'I hope you have nice weather'.
Wetter is
1. singular;
2. a **das** word
3. accusative;
4. the situation is type four.

So you say: **Ich wünsche Ihnen schön*es* Wetter.**

PRACTICE/LEARN BY HEART

Go through the steps above then choose the right answer:

Situation Type One (= adjective alone or after **sein** or **werden**)

You are describing your favourite restaurant:

1. **Es ist...**	It's very cosy.
2. **Das Essen ist...**	The food is good.
3. **Die Kellner sind...**	The waiters are nice.
4. **Es...**	It's not expensive.
5. **Das Bier...**	The beer is cold.
6. **Die Weinkarte...**	The wine list is very good.

gut/kalt/nett/teuer/ganz/gemütlich/sehr gut

Situation Type Two (= der/die/das + adjective + noun)

You are in a shop deciding which clothes you would like to buy:

1. **Ich nehme...**	I'll take the green trousers.
2. **Ich nehme...**	I'll take the white blouse.
3. **Ich nehme...**	I'll take the black jacket.
4. **Ich nehme...**	I'll take the blue shoes.
5. **Ich nehme...**	I'll take the red dress.
6. **Ich nehme...**	I'll take the grey pullover.

Hose/Pullover/Kleid/Bluse/Schuhe/Jacke
den/die/die/die/das/die
grüne/grauen/rote/blauen/schwarze/weiße

Situation Type Three (= **ein/eine** etc. + adjective + noun)
You are trying to decide what to order in a restaurant:

1. **Ich möchte...** I'd like a hot soup.
2. **Ich möchte...** I'd like a light beer.
3. **Ich möchte...** I'd like a black coffee.
4. **Ich möchte...** I'd like a dry white wine.

ein/einen/einen/eine
herben/helles/warme/schwarzen
Kaffee/Bier/Weißwein/Suppe

Situation Type Four (= adjective + noun)
You have gone to the market and are asking if things are available:

1. **Haben Sie...** Have you got fresh milk?
2. **Haben Sie...** Have you got German butter?
3. **Haben Sie...** Have you got new potatoes?
4. **Haben Sie...** Have you got firm tomatoes?
5. **Haben Sie...** Have you got cheap lettuce?
6. **Haben Sie...** Have you got red apples?

Äpfel/Tomaten/Salat/Butter/Milch/Kartoffeln
frische/neue/billigen/rote/feste/deutsche

ANSWERS
Situation One
1. ganz gemütlich 2. gut 3. nett 4. ist nicht teuer 5. ist kalt 6. ist sehr gut
Situation Two
1. die grüne Hose 2. die weiße Bluse 3. die schwarze Jacke 4. die blauen Schuhe 5. das rote Kleid 6. den grauen Pullover
Situation Three
1. eine warme Suppe 2. ein helles Bier 3. einen schwarzen Kaffee 4. einen herben Weißwein
Situation Four
1. frische Milch 2. deutsche Butter 3. neue Kartoffeln 4. feste Tomaten 5. billigen Salat 6. rote Äpfel

Adjective Endings at a glance.

X = noun

1. Situation Type One = adjective alone or after **sein** or **werden**. No endings.
2. Situation Type Two = **der/die/das** + adjective + noun

	der group	**die group**	**das group**	**plural**
Nom.	der ... e X	die ... e X	das ... e X	die ... en Xe
Acc.	den ... en X	die ... e X	das ... e X	die ... en Xe
Dat.	dem ... en X	der ... en X	dem ... en X	den ... en Xen
Gen.	des ... en Xes	der ... en X	des ... en Xes	der ... en Xe

3. Situation Type Three = **ein/kein/mein/Ihr** etc. + adjective + noun

	der group	**die group**	**das group**	**plural**
Nom.	ein ... er X	eine ... e X	ein ... es X	meine ... en Xe
Acc.	einen ... en X	eine ... e X	ein ... es X	meine ... en Xe
Dat.	einem ... en X	einer ... en X	einem ... en X	meinen ... en Xen
Gen.	eines .. en X(e)s	einer ... en X	eines ... en X(e)s	meiner ... en Xe

4. Situation Type Four = adjective + noun

	der group	**die group**	**das group**	**plural**
Nom.	...er X	...e X	...es X	...e Xe
Acc.	...en X	...e X	...es X	...e Xe
Dat.	...em X	...er X	...em X	...en Xen
Gen.	...en X(e)s	...er X	...en X(e)s	...er Xe

Comparison

HOW TO USE

When you compare things in English you say: 'My house is bigg*er than* yours'; 'His car goes fast*er than* ours'; 'Could you speak *more slowly*'. You add '-er' to the adjective if it is short or you put 'more' in front if it is long, and you put 'than' in between the two things you are comparing.

German is very similar but it is simpler because you add **-er** to all adjectives and adverbs, no matter how long they are. For 'than' you say **als**.

Mein Haus ist größ*er als* Ihres.	My house is bigger than yours.
Sein Auto fährt *schneller als* unseres.	His car is faster than ours.
Könnten Sie bitte langsam*er* sprechen?	Could you please speak more slowly?

When you want to compare three or more things in English you say for example:

big, bigg*er*, bigg*est*	**groß, größer, größte**
small, small*er*, small*est*	**klein, kleiner, kleinste**

and as you can see the same thing happens in German: add **-er**, **-(e)ste**.

Ich bin der jüng*ste*.	I am the youngest.
Unser Ältest*er* arbeitet bei der Bank.	Our eldest son works in the bank.

Some points to remember:

1. Most German adjectives and adverbs are quite straightforward and follow the rules above. But there are some very common adjectives which add an Umlaut (¨) so make a note of these:

alt	**älter**	**älteste**	(old, older, oldest)
jung	**jünger**	**jüngste**	(young, younger, youngest)
kalt	**kälter**	**kälteste**	(cold, colder, coldest)
warm	**wärmer**	**wärmste**	(warm/hot, hotter, hottest)
lang	**länger**	**längste**	(long, longer, longest)
kurz	**kürzer**	**kürzeste**	(short, shorter, shortest)

2. Adverbs have no endings, but many of the comparative words are adjectives and must follow the rules about adjective endings.
For example you want to say: 'I'll take the bigger dress'.
Here you add first the comparative ending **-er** to **groß→größer**, then you go through all the steps on page 113.
Kleid is
1. singular;
2. a **das** word;
3. accusative;
4. the situation is type two.

So you say: **Ich nehme *das größere Kleid* bitte.**

You want to say: 'We're looking for a smaller flat'.
Add the comparative ending: **klein→kleiner**.
Wohnung is
1. singular;
2. a **die** word;
3. accusative;
4. the situation type is three.

So you say: **Wir suchen *eine kleinere Wohnung.***

3. We have one or two exceptions in English to the rules. We don't say *good*, *gooder*, *goodest*. Neither do the Germans. Here are the few exceptions:

gut, besser, beste	good, better, best
viel, mehr, meiste	a lot, more, most
hoch, höher, höchste	high, higher, highest

4. To compare two things (as.. as) use **so... wie**:

Unsere Wohnung ist ungefähr *so groß wie* diese.	Our flat is about as big as this one.
Er ist ungefähr *so alt wie* meine Schwester.	He's about as old as my sister.
Mein Auto ist *nicht so schön wie* Ihres.	My car's not as nice as yours.

Adverbs

INTRODUCTION
Adverbs are words which accompany and describe verbs (here, there, loudly, softly etc.). You can say: 'She drives the car'. If you add an adverb, you can say how/when etc. she drives the car:
'She drives the car /badly/well/often/always/sometimes'.

EXPLANATION
To form adverbs in English, you often add '-ly' to the adjective.

beautiful	beautiful*ly*
neat	neat*ly*

German adverbs have no such distinguishing mark. The adjective and the adverb are usually the same word.

Sie ist sehr *schön.*	She/it is very beautiful.
Das ist sehr *schön* gemacht.	That is beautifully done.

But their use is different. The adjective describes a noun or pronoun, the adverb describes a verb.

You can use adverbs to describe:

1. How things are done.
Langsam (slowly), **schnell** (quickly), **schön** (beautifully), **fein** (finely), **gut** (well), **schlecht** (badly) etc.

2. When things are done.
Oft (often), **schon** (already), **manchmal** (sometimes), **sofort** (immediately), **nie** (never), **heute** (today), **immer** (always) etc.

3. Where things are done.
Hier (here), **da drüben** (over there), **oben** (up there), **unten** (underneath), **rechts** (to the right), **links** (to the left) etc.

You can also add comparative endings to adverbs, in the same way as you can to adjectives. Add **-er** ending for 'more'.

Bitte sprechen Sie laut*er*.	Please speak louder.
Bitte sprechen Sie langsam*er*.	Please speak more slowly.

Use **am** + **-sten** ending for 'most'.

***Am schönsten* ist es hier abends.**	It's at its most beautiful here in the evenings.
***Am besten* kommen Sie heute nachmittag vorbei.**	The best thing for you to do is to come round this afternoon.

Possessive adjectives

INTRODUCTION

Possessive adjectives (my, your, his etc.) tell you who owns what, who is related to whom, and are very useful for example when talking about your family and friends or reporting lost property etc. Like all adjectives they describe nouns and their endings are affected by the noun they accompany. They follow the same pattern of endings as **ein** (see p. 97).

EXPLANATION

The possessive adjectives are:

mein	= my	**unser**	= our
dein	= your (familiar singular)	**euer**	= your (familiar plural)
sein	= his/its	**ihr**	= their
ihr	= her/its	**Ihr**	= your (formal)

HOW TO USE

The endings are:

	der group	die group	das group	plural
Nom.	no ending	**-e**	no ending	**-e**
Acc.	**-en**	**-e**	no ending	**-e**
Dat.	**-em**	**-er**	**-em**	**-en**
Gen.	**-es**	**-er**	**-es**	**-er**

Notes.

1. **sein**/(his)/**ihr** (her)

People who speak languages like Spanish and French, where the words for 'his' and 'her' are exactly the same, get confused with **sein** (his) and **ihr** (her). If you find this difficult try the next exercise.

PRACTICE

You are talking about Manfred and Barbara who are very careless and have lost various items. Look up the following nouns in your dictionary and find out which **der/die/das** group they belong to. They are all accusative. Then fill in the blanks with a word for 'his' or 'her'. Use each word only once.

Nouns:
Fotoapparat/Portemonnaie/Rasierapparat/Koffer/Fahrkarte
his/her: **seinen/seinen/sein/ihre/ihren/ihre**

1. **Manfred hat... Rasierapparat verloren.**	Manfred has lost his razor.
2. **Barbara hat... Handtasche verloren.**	Barbara has lost her handbag.
3. **Manfred hat... verloren.**	Manfred has lost his suitcase.
4. **Barbara hat... verloren.**	Barbara has lost her camera.
5. **Manfred hat... verloren.**	Manfred has lost his wallet.
6. **Barbara hat... verloren.**	Barbara has lost her ticket.

2. **ihr** (her)/**ihr** (their)/ **Ihr** (your)

It is often very difficult to distinguish these three meanings when people are speaking because they all sound the same. You really have to have your wits about you! If you didn't follow the conversation, don't pretend you did. Ask **wessen?** (= whose?) and get some clarification as to the person's or people's identity. You will probably be told the person's name and then you will be able to follow the conversation.

LEARN BY HEART

Here are some expressions I hope you won't need! Fill in the correct form of **mein.**

1. **Wo ist... Tasche?**	Where is my bag?
2. **Es tut mir leid, ich habe ... Fahrkarte verloren.**	I'm sorry, I've lost my ticket.
3. **Ich habe ... Portemonnaie zu Hause vergessen.**	I've left my wallet at home.
4. **Ich habe ... Fotoapparat verloren.**	I've lost my camera.
5. **... Auto ist weg!**	My car's gone!
6. **Ich habe ... Uhr vergessen.**	I've forgotten my watch.

And some expressions for dealing with officialdom:

1. **Ist das Ihr Vorname?**	Is that your first name?
2. **Ich habe meinen Paß vergessen.**	I've forgotten my passport.
3. **Wo sind Ihre Papiere?**	Where are your papers?
4. **Ihre Adresse bitte.**	Your address please.
5. **Und Ihre Telefonnummer?**	And your telephone number?

ANSWERS

1st exercise

1. seinen 2. ihre 3 seinen Koffer 4. ihren Fotoapparat
5. sein Portemonnaie 6. ihre Fahrkarte

2nd exercise

1. meine 2. meine 3. mein 4. meinen 5. Mein 6. meine

Some and any

INTRODUCTION

'Some' and 'any' require a bit of careful thought before using them in German.

HOW TO USE

Some

1. 'Some' as an adjective = **manche** + plural noun.

Manche Leute glauben ...	Some people think ...

But miss out the word 'some' entirely when dealing with quantities:

Möchten Sie Brot? Tee?	Would you like some bread?/some tea?

2. 'Some' as a pronoun = **welcher/welche/welches**. Use the same endings as for **der/die/das**.

Brauchen Sie Kartoffeln? Nein, ich habe noch welche.	Do you need potatoes? No, I've still got some.
Im Kühlschrank sind noch welche.	There are some in the fridge.
Möchten Sie welches?	Would you like some of it? (**das** word)
Möchten Sie welchen?	Would you like some of it? (**der** word)

3. Sometimes = **manchmal.**

Manchmal gibt es Schweinefleisch mit Pommesfrites.	Sometimes pork with chips is on the menu.

4. Someone/anyone = **jemand.**

Ist da jemand?	Is someone/anyone there?
Hat jemand angerufen?	Has someone/anyone phoned?
Haben Sie jemand getroffen?	Did you meet someone/anyone?

5. Something = **etwas** or **irgendetwas** (shortened forms: **'was, irgend'was**).

Suchen Sie etwas Bestimmtes?	Are you looking for something in particular?
Etwas stimmt nicht.	There's something wrong.
Ich wollte Ihnen etwas sagen.	I wanted to tell you something.

6. Somehow = **irgendwie.**

Er kommt irgendwie nach Hause.	He'll get home somehow.
Ich habe irgendwie das Gefühl ...	Somehow I've got a feeling that ...

7. Somewhere = **irgendwo.**

Irgendwo auf dem Land.	Somewhere in the country.

8. Sometime = **irgendwann.**

There is a difference in emphasis between words beginning with **irgend-** and the other words for 'some'. **Irgend-** conveys the idea that you don't know, and possibly don't care, who, what, where etc. **Welche, manche, etwas, jemand** etc. are much more definite – you do have a good idea who or what or where you mean.

Any

'Any' has several different uses:

1. When asking whether something is available, miss out the word 'any' in German.

Haben Sie Brot?	Have you any bread?
Gibt es hier Toiletten?	Are there any toilets here?
Haben Sie Kinderschuhe?	Have you any children's shoes?

2. With a negative. Use **kein, nichts** etc. (see p. 71.)

Ich habe kein Brot.	I haven't any bread.
Ich kann mich an nichts erinnern.	I can't remember anything.

3. 'Any' can be vague and indefinite and is very close to 'some'.

Kann ich irgendwo parken?	Is there anywhere (somewhere) I can park?
Wissen Sie etwas über ihn?	Do you know anything (something) about him?

4. 'Any' can be positive, and mean 'all', 'every' etc.

Er kann jeden Tag kommen.	He'll be coming any day now.
Sie können jederzeit zu uns kommen.	Come and see us any time you like.

5. Any time = **jederzeit.**

6. Anybody

jemand	anybody/somebody
Ist da jemand?	Is anybody/somebody there?
niemand	not ... anyone, nobody
jeder	everybody
Jeder kann mitmachen.	Anybody (everybody) can join in.

7. Anywhere

irgendwo	anywhere/somewhere
überall	anywhere/everywhere
Sie können überall parken.	You can park anywhere you like.

8. Anything and everything

etwas, irgendetwas	anything/something (not definite)
Ach, kaufen Sie irgendetwas.	Oh, just buy anything. (I don't care.)
nichts	nothing/not ... anything (see p. 71.)
Ich habe nichts gekauft.	I didn't buy anything.
alles	anything/everything
Hier können Sie alles finden.	You can find anything you're looking for here.
Sie können alles bestellen.	You can order anything you like.

9. Anyhow

irgendwie	anyhow/somehow
auf jeden Fall/sowieso	anyhow/anyway
Das wollte ich sowieso machen.	I wanted to do that anyway.
Wir gehen sowieso ins Theater.	We're going to the theatre anyway.
Auf jeden Fall wollte ich Ihnen alles erklären.	Anyway, I wanted to explain everything to you.

Prepositions

INTRODUCTION

Prepositions are the little words like 'to', 'for', 'with', etc. which we use to indicate for example where, how and when an action is taking place. Although they are very small words, mistakes with prepositions can lead to very big misunderstandings, so do treat them with the respect they deserve. If you can understand the concept behind the preposition you will have an insight into the German person's way of thinking. Where it is helpful, I have included diagrams to illustrate these concepts.

EXPLANATION

Most German prepositions can take the prefixes **wo-** or **da-**. **Wo-** means 'what'/'which' and **da-** means 'it'/'that'. You can use **wo-** with a preposition to make a question. If the preposition begins with a vowel, you insert an extra **-r-**.

auf	on
worauf?	on what?
darauf	on that/it
sprechen über	to talk about
Worüber sprechen Sie?	What are you talking about?
Wir sprachen gerade darüber.	We were just talking about that.

Some prepositions are shortened when they are used with **der/die/das**. For example, **an dem** is shortened to **am**; **bei dem** is shortened to **beim**; **an das** is shortened to **ans** etc.

There are two problems facing us when dealing with German prepositions:

1. Some are followed by the accusative case (see p. 84) and others by the dative case (see p.88) and others by both – so how do we know which takes which?
2. Very often you cannot translate English prepositions directly into their apparent German counterparts. For example, there are at least six different ways of translating 'to'!

1. Prepositions which always take the accusative:

bis	**durch**	**entlang**	**für**	**gegen**	**ohne**	**pro**	**um**
until	through	along	for	against	without	per	about/round

2. Prepositions which always take the dative:

ab	**aus**	**außer**	**bei**	**gegenüber**	**mit**	**nach**	**seit**	**von**	**zu**
from	from	except	at	opposite	with	to/after	for/since	from	to

3. Prepositions which always take the genitive:

aufgrund	**in der Nähe**	**trotz**	**während**	**wegen**
because of	near	in spite of	during	because of

4. Prepositions which take both the accusative and the dative:

an	**auf**	**hinter**	**in**	**neben**	**über**	**unter**	**vor**	**zwischen**
at/ to	at/on/ to	behind	in/ into	near	over/ across	under/ among	before/ ago	between

Why do some prepositions take both the accusative and dative? If you have a closer look you will see that all of the prepositions in this group are connected with *place*. The Germans say that there are two ways of talking about place:

1. Movement from one place to another. The action starts in one place and finishes in another place. To express this idea of movement from A to B

you use verbs of motion, such as **kommen**, **gehen**, **fliegen** (to fly), **einsteigen** (to get into), **stellen** (to put) etc. + one of the prepositions in list number 4 + the accusative.

2. Position in one place, i.e. no movement. To express this idea of no movement you use verbs which describe stationary activities, such as **sein**, **liegen**, **essen**, **trinken**, **stehen** (to stand) etc. + one of the prepositions in list number 4 + the dative.

Let us look at some examples:

In + accusative = in/into/to

Ich fahre in die Stadt.	I'm going into town.
Gehen Sie ins Bett?	Are you going to bed?
Stellen Sie den Wein in den Kühlschrank.	Put the wine in the fridge.

In + dative = in/inside

Er arbeitet in einer Fabrik.	He works in a factory.
Bleiben Sie im Auto.	Stay in the car.
Wir essen im Restaurant.	We'll eat in the restaurant.

In + accusative means you are going into a building/space etc. from a starting point outside. **In** + dative means you are already in the building/space etc. and are staying there.

Warning. We say in English: 'Let's go *to* the cinema/the theatre' etc. It's very tempting to say **zum Kino/zum Theater** etc. But if you say this your German friends will think that for some reason you are not intending to go into the cinema and see the film or into the theatre and watch the play. You seem to want to go to the door of the cinema and then go away again! Says **ins Kino** and **ins Theater**.

An + accusative = to

Wir gehen an den Strand.	We're going to the beach.
Gehen Sie nicht ans Fenster!	Don't go to the window!
Ich schreibe einen Brief an meine Schwester.	I'm writing a letter to my sister.

(Yes, a letter also goes from A to B, even though you don't think of **schreiben** as a verb of movement.)

Bitte hängen Sie das Bild an die Wand.	Please hang the picture on the wall. (on = onto)

An + dative = at/on

Wir haben am Strand gelegen.	We lay on the beach.
Wir saßen noch am Tisch.	We were still sitting at the table.
Ich bin am Bahnhof.	I'm at the station.
Der Zeitungskiosk ist an der Ecke.	The newspaper kiosk is on the corner.

REMINDER

For movement from A→B, use accusative.

For stationary position, [A], use dative.

Auf + accusative = on/onto/to

Stellen Sie die Flasche auf den Tisch.	Put the bottle on the table.
Legen Sie bitte die Zeitung aufs Regal.	Put the newspaper on the shelf please.
Setzen Sie sich bitte auf den Stuhl.	Sit down on the chair please.
Ich gehe auf eine Party.	I'm going to a party.
Ich muß auf die Toilette.	I have to go to the Toilet.

Auf + dative = on/at

Das Buch liegt auf meinem Schreibtisch.	The book is on my desk.
Die Katze ist auf dem Dach.	The cat's on the roof.
Er ist auf der Toilette.	He's at the toilet.
Sie ist auf einer Konferenz.	She's at a conference.

REMINDER ONCE AGAIN:

Movement from A→B	= accusative.
Position in one place [A]	= dative.

Über + accusative = over/across

Wir fahren über die Grenze.	We're going over the border.
Gehen Sie über die Kreuzung.	Go over the crossroads.

Über + dative = over/above

Die Leselampe ist über Ihrem Sitz.	The reading lamp is above your seat.

Have you got the message? This basic difference between movement from A to B (accusative) and position/no movement (dative) applies to all the prepositions in this group.

LEARN BY HEART

You have let your home to some Germans. Here are some instructions and information which you have left for them. Fill in the blanks with a preposition and the appropriate form of **der, die, das.**

1. **Der Fernseher ist ... Wohnzimmer ... ... Ecke.**	The TV is in the living room in the corner.
2. **Die Schlüssel für die Garage liegen ... ... Fernseher.**	The keys for the garage are on the TV.
3. **Milch und Eier sind ... Kühlschrank.**	There are milk and eggs in the fridge.
4. **Um das Telefon zu benutzen, werfen Sie fünf-pence-Stücke ... ... Schlitz.**	To use the telephone, put 5p pieces in the slot.
5. **Bitte tun Sie den Abfall ... Eimer.**	Please put rubbish in the bucket.
6. **Das Fremdenverkehrsamt ist ... ... Saxby Street.**	The tourist office is in Saxby Street.

Now explain to a German visitor how to get to the nearest supermarket:

1. **Fahren Sie ... die Kreuzung.**	Go over the crossroads.
2. **Dann biegen Sie nach rechts ... ... High Street.**	Then turn right into High Street.
3. **Und der Supermarkt ist ... ... Ecke.**	And the supermarket is on the corner.

bei + dative

Warning! **bei** never, never, never means English 'by'!

Use **bei dem** shortened to **beim** for **der/das** words, **bei der** for **die** words.

1. = 'near'

bei der Tankstelle	near the petrol station
Das Hotel liegt ganz nah beim Bahnhof.	The hotel is just next to the station.

ANSWERS

1st exercise

1. im, in der 2. auf dem 3. im 4. in den 5. in den 6. in der

2nd exercise

1. über 2. in die 3. an der

2. – 'during'/'at'

Wir sprechen beim Essen darüber.	We'll talk about that at lunch.

3. = 'given'/'if there is ...' + weather conditions

Bei Gewitter findet das Konzert im Auditorium statt.	If there is a thunderstorm the concert will take place in the auditorium.

4. = 'at'/'in'/'at the house of'/'at so and so's place' (like French *chez*). Use **bei** + where you live, where you work or shop etc., i.e. with the name of the person or company or shop and *not* with a word for a building.

Sie können bei uns wohnen/schlafen.	You can stay with us.
Er wohnt bei seinen Eltern/bei seiner Schwiegermutter/bei Neuraths.	He's staying with his parents/ his mother-in-law/the Neuraths.
bei Schmidt	c/o Schmidt (on letters, also when answering the phone at Schmidt's house. This tells the caller they have the right number and that you are not one of the Schmidts)
Er kauft immer bei Horten ein.	He always shops at Horten (= name of store).
Er arbeitet bei BASF/bei Mercedes etc.	He works at BASF/Mercedes etc.
beim Friseur.	at the hairdresser's.

Notice you can't say: '**Ich bin beim Supermarkt** or name of any building. With a building you must use **in**. You say: **Ich kaufe bei Safeway ein** (name of firm) but: **Ich kaufe im Supermarkt ein** (building). This is a point which English people often make mistakes with.

seit + dative = 'since'/'for'
Seit answers the question **Wie lange?** (how long?).
Be very careful when using **seit**. You use the German present tense to express English 'have been doing' and the imperfect tense to express 'had been doing'. English people find this difficult to grasp, but if you look at it from the German point of view it makes sense: they argue that you are/were still doing the action, so the verb should be present or imperfect.

1. = 'for' + length of time

Ich warte schon seit einer halben Stunde.	I've been waiting for half an hour .
Er wohnt seit drei Jahren in Duisburg.	He's been living in Duisburg for three years.
Er wohnte seit einem Jahr im Haus.	He had been living in the house for a year.

2. = 'since' + specific point in time

Seit meiner Rückkehr bin ich sehr beschäftigt.	I've been very busy since my return.
Er wartet schon seit elf Uhr.	He's been waiting since 11 o'clock.
Ich bin seit gestern wieder hier.	I've been back since yesterday.

ENGLISH PREPOSITIONS

Some English prepositions can be translated directly into German and their use is quite straightforward. Other English prepositions have several different translations in German. The most complicated ones are dealt with here in more detail.

At

1. Saying where you are/live etc.

There is no one word for 'at' in German. Look at these examples:

Ich wohne Friedrichstraße 19.	I live at 19 Friedrichstraße.
Ich bin *beim* Zahnarzt.	I'm at the dentist's.
Ich bin *im* Hotel.	I'm at the hotel.
Ich bin *am* Flughafen.	I'm at the airport.
Ich bin *zu* Hause.	I'm at home.
Ich bin *auf* einer Party.	I'm at a party.

Six different ways of saying 'at', all of them meaning 'at a place'! A German person has a very clear picture in his mind of which word for 'at' is right in each situation. He sees a lot of difference between 'at the airport' and 'at the dentist's'. In order to appreciate this we have to look a little more closely and try to envisage how the German person thinks in this situation. Sometimes it's very difficult for foreigners to understand, so I have listed the most common expressions you are likely to need. If you don't see the logic behind them, forget about any explanation and learn the expressions by heart because you will need them.

1. **Ich wohne Friedrichstraße 19.**
When you give an address, you don't use any word for 'at'.

2. **bei** = at a person's place/on someone's premises. **Bei** is always followed by the dative and you use it with a person or the name of a shop or company. You never use **bei** with a word for a building.

Ich bin beim Friseur.	I'm at the hairdresser's.
Wir schlafen bei meinem Freund.	We are staying at my friend's place.
Ich bin jetzt bei Horten.	I'm at Horten just now (name of shop).

3. **in** + dative = inside a space/building etc. It is used with verbs of position.

Ich bin im Restaurant.	I'm at the restaurant
im Theater	at the theatre
im Kino	at the cinema
im Hotel	at the hotel
im Krankenhaus	at the hospital
Wir sind in der Buchhandlung.	We're at the bookshop
Wir treffen uns in der Fotoabteilung.	We'll meet up in the photographic department
in der Oper	at the opera

4. **An** + dative = at a place, usually referring more to the edge of the building or space than being right inside. It is used with verbs of position.

Die Kinder spielen am Strand.	The children are playing at the beach.
Ich bin jetzt am Flughafen.	I'm at the airport now.
am Bahnhof	at the station
am Fenster	at the window
Ich warte an der Rezeption.	I'm waiting at Reception.
Er ist an der Theke.	He's at the counter/bar.
An der Kreuzung fahren Sie nach rechts.	At the crossroads turn to the right.
an der Ampel	at the traffic lights

5. **Zu Hause**
This is a special expression which you just have to learn. It doesn't belong to any group.

Wir sind jetzt zu Hause.	We're at home now.

6. **auf** + dative
This is used with a small number of nouns. The best thing is to learn them by heart because there is no real explanation why this particular group of nouns takes **auf**.

auf einer Konferenz	at a conference
auf der Messe	at the trade fair
auf der Toilette	at the toilet
auf einer Party	at a party
auf der Bank	at the bank
auf der Post	at the Post Office

In addition to all these ways of saying 'at a place', there are some other ways of saying 'at':

7. **vor** + dative = in front of.

Das Auto steht vor der Tür.	The car's at the door.

8. For 'at' + expressions of time use **um**:

um Viertel vor acht	at quarter to eight
um Mitternacht	at midnight
um sechszehn Uhr dreißig	at 16.30

By

Never translate 'by' with the German word **bei**.

1. **von** = action done by someone. Use the dative after **von**.

Das Buch wurde von Agatha Christie geschrieben.	The book was written by Agatha Christie.

2. **mit** + dative = by + means of transport.

Wir sind mit dem Zug gekommen.	We came by train.
mit dem Auto	by car
mit dem Bus	by bus
mit der U-Bahn	by underground

3. For 'by' + time reference use **um, vor, bis**:

Wir müssen bis zwanzig Uhr zurück sein.	We must be back by 8 pm.
Wir wollen um vier Uhr in der Stadt sein.	We want to be in the town by four o'clock.
Das müssen wir vor morgen fertig haben.	We have to have it ready by tomorrow.

4. **mit** + dative

Kann ich mit Scheck bezahlen?	Can I pay by cheque?
Das ist mit der Hand geschrieben.	It's written by hand.
Das schicke ich mit der nächsten Post.	I'll send it by the next post.

5. **aus**

aus Versehen	by mistake

Near

There is no single translation of our preposition 'near'. The best way to translate 'near' is to use one of the following expressions:

1. **in der Nähe von** + dative = in the vicinity of/ near:

Wir wohnen in der Nähe vom Bahnhof.	We are staying near the station.
Das Hotel liegt in der Nähe vom Flughafen.	The hotel is near the airport.

You can also use **in der Nähe** with the genitive:

Wir wohnen in der Nähe der Oxford Street.	We are staying near Oxford Street.

Notice the use of **der** with the street name.

2. **nicht weit von** + dative = not far from.

Wir wohnen nicht weit von der Stadtmitte.	We are staying near the town centre.
Das ist nicht weit von meinem Hotel.	That's near my hotel.

3. **neben** + dative/accusative = near/next to.

Neben can only be used with places which are very close to each other. Use the dative when describing position and the accusative when there is movement towards one of the places.

Die Toiletten sind neben der Treppe.	The toilets are next to the stairs.
Stellen Sie bitte den Koffer neben den Wagen.	Please put the case next to the car.

4. **bei** + dative = near/at/around.

Bei der Tankstelle biegen Sie nach links.	Near the petrol station take a left turn.
Ich wohne beim Flughafen.	I live near the airport.

To

1. Saying where you are going to.
There is no one word for 'to' in German. Look at these examples:

Wir fahren morgen nach Newcastle.	We're going to Newcastle tomorrow.
Ich gehe jetzt ins Büro.	I'm going to the office now.
Fahren Sie zum Flughafen?	Are you going to the airport?
Wollen wir an den Strand gehen?	Shall we go to the beach?
Wir sind auf eine Party eingeladen.	We're invited to a party.

Five different ways of saying 'to', all of them meaning movement towards a place!

A German person has a very clear picture in his mind of which word for 'to' is right in each situation. He sees a lot of difference between 'to the office' and 'to the airport'.

1. **nach** + name of a town or country = to.
Don't use **nach** with countries which begin with the definite article (**der/die/das**) – use **in** + accusative for them (see point no. 2).

Wann fahren Sie nach Schweden?	When are you going to Sweden?
Ich fahre übermorgen nach Cardiff.	I'm going to Cardiff the day after tomorrow.

nach London, nach Edinburgh, nach Bonn, nach Deutschland etc.

2. **in** + accusative.
Use this when 'to' really means 'into'. You are going into a different building/space etc. It is also used for the few countries which begin with **der/die/das**:

Wir fahren in die Schweiz/in die Türkei/in die Bundesrepublik/in die DDR/.	We're going to Switzerland/Turkey/The Federal Republic of Germany/The German Democratic Republic/.
Gehen wir ins Kino/ins Konzert/ins Hotel/ins Theater/ins Freibad.	Let's go to the cinema/to the concert/to the hotel/to the theatre/to the swimming pool.
Ich gehe jetzt ins Bett.	I'm going to bed now.
Fahren Sie in die Stadt?	Are you going to town?

3. **zu** + dative

Zu focuses more on the journey to your destination than the actual going inside. If you say **Ich fahre zum Flughafen**, you mean you are driving to the airport and you might go into the building as well. If you say **Ich fahre in den Flughafen**, you mean you are driving your vehicle right into the airport building (which might have disastrous results!).

Zum Flughafen bitte!	To the airport please! (Taxi)
Fahren Sie zum Bahnhof?	Are you going to the station?
Fährt dieser Bus zum Zoo/zum Theater/zum Hallenbad/?	Does this bus go to the zoo/the theatre/the indoor swimming pool/?
Wie weit ist es zur nächsten Haltestelle?	How far is it to the next bus stop?
Gehen Sie bitte zum Schalter drei/zur Kasse.	Please go to counter number three/to the cash desk.
Ich gehe jetzt zum Bäcker/zu Hertie.	I'm going to the baker's now/to Hertie (name of store).
Ich gehe jetzt zu meinem Freund.	I'm going to my boyfriend's place.
Wie weit ist es zur Schillerstraße?	How far is it to Schillerstraße?

Notice that in German you use **die** etc. with street names.

4. **an** + accusative.

An implies going to the edge of a building/space etc. rather than going right inside it. When you say **Wir fahren ans Meer**, you mean 'we're going to the seaside' (i.e. the edge of the sea) rather than plunging into the sea in your car.

Kommen Sie bitte ans Fenster.	Come to the window please.
Der Kellner kommt an Ihren Tisch.	The waiter comes to your table.
Wollen wir an den Strand heute?	Shall we go to the beach today?
Wir fahren ans Meer.	We're going to the seaside.

5. **auf** + accusative.

This is used with a small number of nouns. The best thing is to learn them by heart because there is no real explanation why this particular group of nouns takes **auf**.

Ich gehe auf eine Konferenz.	I'm going to a conference.
Ich gehe auf die Messe/auf die Bank/auf die Post/auf die Toilette/aufs Klo.	I'm going to the trade fair/to the bank/to the Post Office/to the toilet/to the loo.
Ich gehe auf eine Party.	I'm going to a party.

In addition to these various ways of saying ‘to a place’, there are some more expressions with ‘to’:

6. Vor + time

zehn Minuten vor acht	ten minutes to eight
viertel vor neun	a quarter to nine

7. von ... bis = from ... to.

Das Museum ist von zehn bis fünfzehn Uhr geöffnet	The museum is open from 10am to 3pm.

Numbers

INTRODUCTION

Numbers are quite easy to deal with as long as you can see them written down, but unfortunately for much of the time you will find yourself having to understand and give numbers aloud. Think of all the information you hear which contains numbers – times, prices, sizes, dates, addresses, quantities and so on. If you don't have a thorough knowledge of spoken numbers you could end up paying DM15 instead of DM5 or missing the train because it left at 16.30 not 17.30. The possibilities are endless!

You will also need numbers when giving or asking for personal information such as birthdays, telephone numbers, addresses etc.

Since numbers perform such a key role in so many situations, it's worth taking the time to learn and practise them aloud for yourself.

HOW TO USE

The German number system is similar to our own and is quite logical, so try to see the parallels which exist between English and German – they will help you to learn.

There are two kinds of numbers:

1. *Cardinal numbers*, e.g. one, two, three etc. They describe quantity, how many.
2. *Ordinal numbers*, e.g. first, second, third etc. They describe the order of things in a system.

Cardinal Numbers

0–19 **(null bis neunzehn)**

0	**null**	7	**sieben**
1	**eins**	8	**acht**
2	**zwei**	9	**neun**
3	**drei**	10	**zehn**
4	**vier**	11	**elf**
5	**fünf**	12	**zwölf**
6	**sechs**	13	**dreizehn**

14	**vierzehn**	17	**siebzehn**
15	**fünfzehn**	18	**achtzehn**
16	**sechszehn**	19	**neunzehn**

From 0–19 the German numbers are parallel to English. From 13–19 (**dreizehn bis neunzehn**) the **-zehn** ending is the same as our *-teen* ending in 'thir*teen*' etc. Be sure to say the **-zehn** ending really clearly, so you don't get **neunzehn** (19) confused with **neunzig** (90). Most people learning German mumble because they're not quite sure, but this is a case where mumbling can get you into trouble. Here it's essential to be *absolutely sure*. If you're not sure, write down the figure and show it to the other person.

20–99	**(zwanzig bis neunundneunzig)**		
20	**zwanzig**	40	**vierzig**
21	**einundzwanzig**	41	**einundvierzig**
22	**zweiundzwanzig**	50	**fünfzig**
23	**dreiundzwanzig**	51	**einundfünfzig**
24	**vierundzwanzig**	60	**sechszig**
25	**fünfundzwanzig**	61	**einundsechszig**
26	**sechsundzwanzig**	70	**siebzig**
27	**siebenundzwanzig**	71	**einundsiebzig**
28	**achtundzwanzig**	80	**achtzig**
29	**neunundzwanzig**	81	**einundachtzig**
30	**dreißig**	90	**neunzig**
31	**einunddreißig**	99	**neunundneunzig**

From 20–99 there are three points to notice:
1. **Sieben** gets slightly shortened in **siebzehn/siebzig**.
2. Our *-ty* ending in *forty* etc. is echoed by the German **-zig in vierzig** etc. (but note: **dreißig**). Make sure you say the **-zig/ßig** ending clearly.
3. Instead of saying *twenty-one*, Germans say *one-and-twenty*. Think of 'four and twenty blackbirds' and you'll keep right.

Warning! Numbers need a lot of practice, especially writing down numbers spoken aloud. Many people find it helps to write down numbers between 20 and 99 from right to left because this is the order in which the Germans say them.

PRACTICE

Write down the following numbers in figures:

1. **Neununddreißig**
2. **dreiundvierzig**
3. **fünfundfünfzig**
4. **fünfundvierzig**
5. **einundzwanzig**
6. **fünfzehn**
7. **vierundfünfzig**
8. **sechsundsiebzig**

HOW TO USE

Over 100

100	**hundert**
101	**hunderteins**
102	**hundertzwei**
103	**hundertdrei**
120	**hundertzwanzig**
136	**hundertsechsunddreißig**
147	**hundertsiebenundvierzig**
179	**hundertneunundsiebzig**
200	**zweihundert**
265	**zweihundertfünfundsechszig**
300	**dreihundert**
400	**vierhundert**
500	**fünfhundert**
600	**sechshundert**
700	**siebenhundert**
1,000	**tausend**
1,100	**tausendeinhundert**
2,000	**zweitausend**
5,000	**fünftausend**
10,000	**zehntausend**
100,000	**hunderttausend**
1,000,000	**eine Million**

Although these words look long, this is only because all the numbers are written together. 121 is just as much of a mouthful to say in English as it is in German. Whereas in English we say 'one hundred and twenty-one', the Germans say 'one hundred one and twenty': **einhunderteinundzwanzig**. The 'and' is in a different place, but it takes just as long to say.

ANSWERS

1. 39; 2. 43; 3. 55; 4. 45; 5. 21; 6. 15; 7. 54; 8. 76

Some useful abbreviations you might come across with numbers:
Mio. = **Million**
Mrd. = **Milliarde** (1000 million)
Nr. = **Nummer**
ca. = **circa/zirka** (approx.)

Some words which often accompany numbers:
ungefähr, rund, zirka (ca.) all mean 'about, approximately'.

über	more than
weniger als	less than, fewer than
knapp	just under
knapp hundert Gramm	just under 100 grams (98 or so)
knapp sechszig Leute	just under 60 people (58 or 59)

English decimal points are represented by commas in German:
5,2 **fünf komma zwei**
0,4 **null komma vier**
0,18 **null komma eins acht**

Percent = **Prozent**
6,2% **sechs komma zwei Prozent**
8,9% **acht komma neun Prozent**

The comma in English thousands is represented in German by a space:
10 000 **zehntausend**
21 456 **einundzwanzigtausendvierhundertsechsundfünfzig**

Fractions

die Hälfte	half
ein Drittel	a third
ein Viertel	a quarter
ein Fünftel	a fifth
ein Sechstel	a sixth etc.

Note: These are all **das** words except for **die Hälfte.**

anderthalb	one and a half
zweieinhalb	two and a half
dreieinhalb	three and a half
viereinhalb	four and a half etc.

Once, twice, thrice etc.

einmal	once
zweimal	twice
dreimal	three times
viermal	four times
hundertmal	a hundred times
x-mal / **-zigmal**	hundreds (lots) of times

Ich habe ihm -zigmal gesagt, er sollte das Rauchen aufgeben. I've told him time and time again to give up smoking.

PRACTICE

Here is Frau Lange telling you about herself. Write down the numbers in the English translation.

1. **Ich bin achtundvierzig Jahre alt.**	I am … years old.
2. **Meine Telefonnummer ist sechszig, neunzehn, neunundzwanzig.**	My telephone number is …
3. **Ich wohne Hardenbergstraße dreiundvierzig.**	I live at … Hardenbergstraße.
4. **Ich habe zwei Söhne und eine Tochter.**	I have … sons and a daughter.
5. **Michael ist achtzehn Jahre alt und Günther ist einundzwanzig.**	Michael is … and Günther is … years old.
6. **Meine Tochter Anna ist vierundzwanzig Jahre alt.**	My daughter Anna is … years old.
7. **Ich trage Kleidergröße vierzig und Schuhgröße neununddreißig.**	I take size … in clothes and shoe size …
8. **Ich wiege dreiundfünfzig Kilo und bin ein Meter sechszig groß.**	I weigh … kilos and am … tall.
9. **Ich verdiene zweitausend dreihundert Mark im Monat.**	I earn … Marks a month.

Now try to give the same information about yourself and your family.

ANSWERS

1. 48; 2. 60 19 29; 3. 43; 4. 2; 5. 18, 21; 6. 24; 7. 40, 39; 8. 53, 1 metre 60 cms; 9. 2,300.

Ordinal Numbers

INTRODUCTION

You can expect to use or hear ordinal numbers with dates, directions (floors or storeys in a building, which street, room etc.), asking for tickets (1st, 2nd class), on a guided tour (which king, which century etc.) and so on.

EXPLANATION

It is important to remember that ordinal numbers are adjectives and follow the rules governing adjective endings (see p. 110). So you must be clear whether the noun they accompany is:

1. singular/plural;
2. **der/die/das;**
3. nominative/accusative/dative/genitive;
4. situation type 1/2/3/4.

You will usually find ordinal numbers with situation type 2 (with **der/die/das**).

HOW TO USE

Most ordinal numbers are formed quite simply from the cardinal numbers (see p. 139). The rule is: for numbers from 1–19 add **-te** to the cardinal number; from 20 upward add **-ste** to the cardinal number.

However, there are one or two exceptions. Just as in English, *one* does not go to *oneth*, so in German you have:

erste	first
zweite	second
dritte	third

Numbers involving **sieben** are shortened: **sieb** + ending.

1st	**erste**
2nd	**zweite**
3rd	**dritte**
4th	**vierte**
5th	**fünfte**
6th	**sechste**
7th	**siebte**
8th	**achte**
9th	**neunte**
10th	**zehnte**

11th	**elfte**
12th	**zwölfte**
13th	**dreizehnte**
14th	**vierzehnte**
20th	**zwanzigste**
21st	**einundzwanzigste**
22nd	**zweiundzwanzigste**
30th	**dreißigste**
99th	**neunundneunzigste**
100th	**hundertste**

LEARN BY HEART

Here are some examples you will see, hear or use yourself.

(In a guided tour)

written form	spoken form	English
Heinrich VIII.	**Heinrich der Achte.**	Henry the Eighth.
Das Schloß wurde von Ludwig II erbaut.	**Das Schloß wurde von Ludwig dem Zweiten erbaut.**	The castle was built by Ludwig the Second.
(In a hotel or shop)		
Ihr Zimmer ist im 5. Stock/ in der 5. Etage.	**Ihr Zimmer ist im fünften Stock/ in der fünften Etage.**	Your room is on the fifth floor.
Die Schuhabteilung ist im 3. Stock.	**Die Schuhabteilung ist im dritten Stock.**	The shoe department is on the third floor.
(Tickets)		
Einmal 2. Klasse bitte.	**Einmal zweite Klasse bitte.**	One second class ticket please.
(Dates)		
Wir kommen vom 28. April–15 Mai.	**Wir kommen vom achtundzwanzigsten April bis zum fünfzehnten Mai.**	We're coming from the 28th April to the 15th May.

Notice that when you write the short form **1. Stock** etc. you must put a fullstop after the number. There is no short ending to correspond with our 1*st*, 2*nd* etc.

Dates

EXPLANATION

There are four things you need to know before you can say or understand dates in German:

1. days of the week (see p.151);
2. months (see p.152);
3. ordinal numbers (see p.144);
4. years.

HOW TO USE

1. To say today's date, use **sein** (to be) + **der** + **-e** ending. When using ordinal numbers, remember that they are adjectives and take endings. If you want to say: 'Today's the 15th June', the date is nominative after the verb **sein** (see p.82). So you say: **Heute ist d*er* fünfzehnt*e* Juni.**

2. For dates in letters, with signatures etc. use **den** + **-en** ending (= accusative). There are several ways of writing the date but they are all spoken aloud in the same way:

written: **den 27. April 1982**
den 27.04.82
aloud: **den siebenundzwanzigsten April neunzehnhundertzweiundachtzig.**

Sometimes instead of **April** you will also hear **vierten** (= 4th month): **den siebenundzwanzigsten vierten**. There is no word for *of* as in 'fifth *of* June'. Remember always to put a full stop after the number.

3. For dates with prepositions, 'from ... to', 'on the ...' and so on the way to say *on* a certain date is **am** + **-en** ending (=dative).

am zweiten Januar	on the second of January
am sechsten Mai	on the sixth of May

The way to say *from* one date *to* another is **vom** + **-en** ending, **bis zum** + **-en** ending.

Ich möchte ein Zimmer vom zehnten August bis zum ersten September.	I'd like a room from the 10th August to the 1st September.
Ich bin vom vierten siebten bis zum zwanzigsten siebten im Urlaub.	I'm on holiday from the 4th to the 20th July.

4. Years
1926 = **neunzehnhundertsechsundzwanzig**
1955 = **neunzehnhundertfünfundfünfzig**
It's quite straightforward. Split the year into two sections and remember to say **hundert** in the middle.

Important: when talking about years in dates, don't add *in*. In English we say: 'I was born *in* 1953'. In German it is: **Ich bin 1953 geboren.**

PRACTICE/LEARN BY HEART
Now write down some information about yourself, using days, months and years in full, e.g. when your birthday is; when you're going on holiday; when you started learning German etc.

Time

INTRODUCTION

Time is one area where you can't get away with bluffing. You have to make sure you have understood exactly what the other person has said, so if you are in any doubt ask them to repeat it, write it down, or even say it in English:

Könnten Sie das bitte	**wiederholen?**	Could you please	repeat that?
	aufschreiben?		write it down?
	auf Englisch sagen?		say it in English?

And if you still don't understand, say so!

Es tut mir leid, ich verstehe nicht. Sorry, I don't understand.

HOW TO USE

You need to be able to use and understand:

1. The everyday expressions of time used in conversation.

Question:	**Wie spät ist es?** / **Wieviel Uhr ist es?**	What time is it?
Answer:	**Es ist ...**	It's ...

Uhr = o'clock

Zehn Uhr	10 o'clock
Acht Uhr	8 o'clock

Viertel vor = a quarter to

Viertel vor eins	A quarter to one

Viertel nach = a quarter past

Viertel nach sieben	A quarter past seven

Notice that **Viertel** has a capital letter because it is a noun.

halb = half. Warning! **halb** needs special attention. Always stop and think when someone says **halb**:

Es ist halb *elf*.	It is half past *ten*.	10.30

Germans say it is 'half way towards eleven o'clock', whereas in English we think of it as being half way after ten o'clock. We are both correct, but express the idea differently.

Here are some more examples:

Es ist halb neun.	It is half past eight.	8.30
Es ist halb zwei.	It is half past one.	1.30

Now you try:

1. **Es ist halb eins.** ....
2. **Es ist halb elf.** ....
3. **Es ist halb acht.** ....
4. **Es ist halb zwölf.** ....

Other times

Vor = before **nach** = after, past

Es ist zwanzig Minuten vor neun.	It is twenty to nine.
Es ist elf Minuten vor zehn.	It is eleven minutes to ten.
Es ist zehn Minuten nach acht.	It is ten past eight.
Es ist dreizehn Minuten nach drei.	It is thirteen minutes past three.

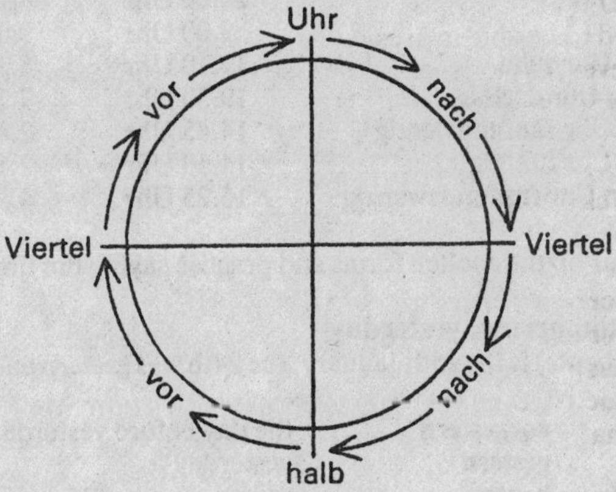

Question:	**Um wieviel Uhr?** / **Wann?**	When?
Answer:	**Um** + time	at ...
um zwanzig vor zehn		at twenty to ten
um halb sechs		at half past five
um Viertel nach zwölf		at a quarter past twelve

ANSWERS

1. 12.30 2. 10.30 3. 7.30 4. 11.30

PRACTICE

Fill in the time:

1. **Ich komme um zwanzig vor acht.**	I'll be there at ...
2. **Ich komme um halb zehn.**	I'll be there at ...
3. **Ich komme um zehn nach sieben.**	I'll be there at ...
4. **Ich komme um Viertel vor zwei.**	I'll be there at ...
5. **Ich komme um halb eins.**	I'll be there at ...
6. **Ich komme um neun Minuten vor elf.**	I'll be there at ...

If you use this system it is sometimes not clear whether **acht Uhr** means 8 o'clock in the morning or in the evening. In this case you will need to use the 24-hour clock, which is used in stations and airports, time-tables, the speaking clock, for opening times, entertainments etc.

spoken	*written*	*English*
zwanzig Uhr	20.00 Uhr	8pm
neun Uhr	9.00 Uhr	9am
siebzehn Uhr zehn	17.10 Uhr	5.10pm
neunzehn Uhr dreißig	19.30 Uhr	7.30pm
vierzehn Uhr fünfundvierzig	14.45 Uhr	2.45pm
vierzehn Uhr fünfzig	14.50 Uhr	2.50pm
sechszehn Uhr fünfundzwanzig	16.25 Uhr	4.25pm

Now cover up the spoken forms and practise saying the time aloud.

Today, tomorrow, yesterday

If today (**heute**) is the 25th January, the 24th was **gestern** and the 26th is **morgen**.

23. Jan	**vorgestern**	the day before yesterday
24. Jan	**gestern**	yesterday
25. Jan	**heute**	today
26. Jan	**morgen**	tomorrow
27. Jan	**übermorgen**	the day after tomorrow

ANSWERS

1. twenty to eight 2. half past nine 3. ten past seven 4. a quarter to two 5. half past twelve 6. nine minutes to eleven

You can combine these expressions with the parts of the day to specify times:

morgen abend	tomorrow evening
heute morgen	this morning
gestern nachmittag	yesterday afternoon
vorgestern abend	the evening before yesterday
heute mittag	today at lunchtime

Although **morgen** means both 'tomorrow' and 'morning', it is nearly always clear which is meant. You never say **morgen morgen**. 'Tomorrow morning' is expressed by the phrase **morgen früh**.

PRACTICE

Someone is suggesting times when you could meet. Write down the English.

1. **morgen früh um acht Uhr**
2. **morgen nachmittag um Viertel nach zwei**
3. **übermorgen um zwanzig Uhr fünfundvierzig**
4. **heute abend um halb sieben**
5. **morgen abend um zwanzig vor zehn**
6. **heute nachmittag um drei**

Days of the week

The difficult ones to remember are **Dienstag** and **Donnerstag**, so give them some extra attention.

Day	*Abbreviation*	*English*
Sonntag	**So.**	Sunday
Montag	**Mo.**	Monday
Dienstag	**Di.**	Tuesday
Mittwoch	**Mi.**	Wednesday
Donnerstag	**Do.**	Thursday
Freitag	**Fr.**	Friday
Samstag (**Sonnabend**)	**Sa.**	Saturday

ANSWERS

1. 8a.m. tomorrow morning 2. 2.15 tomorrow afternoon 3. 8.45p.m. the day after tomorrow 4. half past six this evening 5. 9.40p.m. tomorrow evening 6. 3p.m. this afternoon

Months

Januar, Februar, März, April, Mai, Juni, Juli, August, September, Oktober, November, Dezember.

Sometimes, especially on the phone, it is not clear whether someone has said **Juni** or **Juli**, so you pronounce them: **Juni** ('yoonee' to rhyme with 'see'), **Juli** ('yooly' to rhyme with 'sky').

im Juni	in June

Wordbuilding

INTRODUCTION

If you like playing with words or you want to have a clearer insight into the system behind German word formation, it is worth spending some time reading this section. It will help you:

1. To decode the seemingly endless long words in German. If you regard these as a challenge, you will really enjoy breaking them down and working out their meaning. You will discover that you have unlocked a very powerful door.
2. To make up your own German words. You'll never be stuck for words again! Try taking an English word, add a suitable prefix or ending, and make it sound German. More often than not, people will understand you. They may even marvel at your sophisticated vocabulary!

EXPLANATION

The first group of words we look at are *nouns*.

1. You can put two nouns together:

Zehnmarkschein	a ten Mark note
Gepäckannahme	luggage registration/left luggage
Wetterbericht	weather report
Studentenausweis	student ID card

In English we put two nouns together as well, but we still write them as separate words. The only difference with German is that the words are all written together in one word. If you write two nouns together in German, the last noun determines which **der/die/das** group the whole word belongs to: **Stadtzentrum = die Stadt + das Zentrum**, so **das Stadtzentrum**.

So, be bold! If you find yourself writing **Winter Sport** in German, – write them as one word! **Wintersport**. It looks so much more German.

2. You can join a verb with a noun:

Wartezimmer	waiting room
Kochtopf	cooking pot

3. You can join an adjective with a noun:

Großstadt	big town
Rotwein	red wine
Weißwein	white wine

4. There are all sorts of prefixes you can put on the beginning of nouns. Here are some of the most useful:

Haupt- (= main)	**Hauptbahnhof**	main station
	Hauptsaison	high season
	Haupteingang	main entrance
Neben- (= less important)	**Nebenstraße**	side street
	Nebensaison	low season
Sonder- (= special)	**Sonderangebot**	special offer
	Sonderfahrt	special trip
Lieblings- (= favourite)	**Lieblingskuchen**	favourite cake
	Lieblingsfarbe	favourite colour
	Lieblingsessen	favourite food
Außen- (= outside)	**Außenpolitik**	foreign policy
	Außentemperatur	temperature outside
	Außenminister	Foreign Minister
Innen- (= inside)	**Innenpolitik**	domestic policy
	Innenraum	inside space
	Innenminister	Minister for Home Affairs
Nord- (= North)	**Norddeutschland**	North Germany
Süd- (= South)	**Südwestengland**	South West England etc.
West- (= West)		
Ost- (= East)		
Gesamt- (= total)	**Gesamtbetrag**	total sum
	Gesamtzahl	total number
	Gesamtpreis	total price
Höchst- (= maximum)	**Höchstpreis**	maximum price
	Höchstgeschwindigkeit	maximum speed limit
	Höchsttemperatur	maximum temperature
Mindest- (= minimum)	**Mindestpreis**	lowest price
	Mindestalter	minimum age

Not- (= emergency)	**Notstand**	state of emergency
	Notfall	emergency case
	Notarzt	emergency doctor
Fern- (= long distance)	**Fernseher**	television
	Fernsprecher	telephone
	Ferngespräch	long distance call

You will have noticed that German seems to specialise in very long words like: **Lebensmittelabteilung**, **Geschirrspülmaschine**, **Frühstücksteller**, **Anmeldeformular etc.** This all looks very daunting at first, but once you know the simple rules it becomes much clearer.

Next time you see a long word, remember that it can be broken down into smaller units. Take **Lebensmittelabteilung. Abteilung** = department, **Leben** = life, **Mittel** = means. So it's the 'department for the means of life', which is the food department.
Geschirrspülmaschine. Geschirr = crockery, **spülen** = to wash, rinse, **Maschine** = machine. So it's a dishwasher.
Frühstücksteller. Teller = plate, **früh** = early, **Stück** = bit, piece, **Früstück** = breakfast. So it's a breakfast plate.
Anmeldeformular. Anmelden = to register, **Formular** = a form. So it's a registration form.
Here are a few more for you to try.

1. **Staubsauger**
2. **Mittagessen**
3. **Zimmervermittlung**
4. **Fernsehapparat**
5. **Autobahngaststätte**
6. **Rasierklinge**

So you see it can be fun! Next time you see a long German word, don't cringe. Regard it as a challenge and see if you can crack the code. And remember – you can have a go at making your own long words too.

Adjectives can also be put together:

hellblau	light blue
dunkelrot	dark red
schwarzweiß	black and white (photos etc.)

ANSWERS

1. vacuum cleaner 2. lunch 3. hotel reservations office 4. television 5. motorway restaurant 6. razor blade

Verbs

Here are some very common prefixes for verbs:

ab-	= away
abmachen	undo
abnehmen	take away, lose weight
auf-	= up
aufsteigen	climb up
aufstellen	put up, (e.g. tent etc.)
auf-	= open
aufmachen	to open
aufdrehen	to unscrew
aufschließen	to open
aus-	= movement out
ausgehen	to go out
aussteigen	to get out of vehicle
durch-	= through
durchgehen, durchfahren	to go through
ein-	= movement in
einlaufen	to shrink
einwerfen	to post, (literally 'throw in')
einsteigen	to get in (vehicle)
her-	= towards the speaker away from somewhere else
herbringen	to bring over here
herholen	to fetch from somewhere else etc.
hin-	= away from you towards something else
hinlaufen	to go towards something
hinlegen	to put something down over there
hinhängen	to hang something up over there
mit-	= with
mitfahren	to get a lift
mitnehmen	to take away with you etc.
vorbei-	= past
vorbeigehen, vorbeifahren	to go past
weg-	= away
wegwerfen	to throw away
weggehen	to go away
weiter-	= further on – direction

weitergehen, weiterfahren	to keep going
weiter-	= continue doing something
weitermachen	to carry on doing
wieder-	= again
wiedersehen	to see again
wiederholen	to repeat
wiederhören	to hear again
wieder-	= back
wiederkommen	to come back
wiedergeben	to give back
zurück-	= back
zurückfahren	to go back
zurückkommen	to come back
zurückrufen	to call back (phone etc.)
zu-	= closed
zumachen	to close
zudrehen	to screw shut

Word endings

1. Nouns

-in for female jobs, nationality:

Reiseleiterin	courier
Studentin	female student
Engländerin	lady from England

-er for male jobs, nationality:

Bäcker	baker
Politiker	politician
Amerikaner	man from America
Berliner	man from Berlin etc.

-chen and **-lein** for a small version of something:

Brot	bread
Brötchen	bread roll
Paket	packet
Päkchen	small packet
Buch	book
Büchlein	booklet

-ei for shops, workshops, factories

Bäckerei	bakery
Metzgerei	butcher's
Molkerei	dairy

(added to an adjective) **-heit**:

Sicherheit	safety
Schönheit	beauty

(added to an adjective) **-keit**:

Möglichkeit	possibility

(added to an adjective) **-igkeit**:

Müdigkeit	tiredness
Arbeitslosigkeit	unemployment
Geschwindigkeit	speed

(derived from a verb) **-ung**:

Mitteilung	message
Anmeldung	reception desk
Rechnung	bill
Störung	fault, disturbance

2. Adjectives

Noun + **-lich**:

freundlich	friendly
wissenschaftlich	scientific
jährlich	annual

Noun + **-ig** (similar to '-y' in English):

salzig	salty
durstig	thirsty
giftig	poisonous

Noun + **isch** for nationality:

österreichisch	Austrian
griechisch	Greek
europäisch	European

Noun + **-los** (similar to '-less' in English):

arbeitslos	unemployed (literally 'without work')
hoffnungslos	hopeless
problemlos	without problem

Verb + **-bar** (similar to '-able' in English):

machbar	feasible
waschbar	washable
eßbar	edible

un- + adj. (negative)

ungenießbar	inedible, 'off'
unmöglich	impossible
ungesund	unhealthy

3. Verbs

If you're stuck for a verb in German, take the English word, add **-ieren**, and give it a strong German pronunciation. More often than not, people will understand you or tell you the real German word for it.

studieren	study
spezialisieren	specialise
organisieren	organise
telefonieren	telephone
diskutieren	discuss
profitieren	profit
diktieren	dictate
kritisieren	criticise

PRACTICE

Here are some signs which you will come across in German streets, stations, transport, which might have baffled you up to now. See if you can work them out.

1. KEINE DURCHFAHRT
2. BAHNHOFSMISSION
3. NICHTRAUCHER
4. STADTRUNDFAHRT
5. REISEZUGAUSKUNFT
6. ABFAHRT DER FERNZÜGE
7. EINBAHNSTRASSE
8. NOTAUSSTIEG
9. SPEISEWAGEN
10. SCHLIESSFÄCHER
11. MIETWAGEN
12. NICHT EINSTEIGEN
13. HALTESTELLE
14. VERKEHRSAMT

Next time you are in Germany, make your own list of signs. You'll be surprised how much more you understand about your surroundings.

ANSWERS

1. No Through Road 2. Station Charity 3. Non-Smoker 4. City Tour 5. Train Information 6. Departures, long-distance trains 7. One-way Street 8. Emergency Exit 9. Dining Car 10. Luggage Lockers 11. Car-hire 12. Do not get in 13. Bus Stop 14. Tourist Office

Grammar patterns

An overview of German grammar endings to help you see the connections.

1. masculine

	the	who?	he/him it	a	your	no	endings
Nom.	der	wer?	er	ein	Ihr	kein	**-r** or none
Acc.	den	wen?	ihn	einen	Ihren	keinen	**-n**
Dat.	dem	wem?	ihm	einem	Ihrem	keinem	**-m**

2. feminine

	the	she/her it	a	your	no	endings
Nom.	die	sie	eine	Ihre	keine	**-e**
Acc.	die	sie	eine	Ihre	keine	**-e**
Dat.	der	ihr	einer	Ihrer	keiner	**-r**

3. neuter

	the	it	a	your	no	endings
Nom.	das	es	ein	Ihr	kein	**-s** or none
Acc.	das	es	ein	Ihr	kein	**-s** or none
Dat.	dem	ihm	einem	Ihrem	keinem	**-m**

4. plural

	the	they/them	your	no	endings
Nom.	die	sie	Ihre	keine	**-e**
Acc.	die	sie	Ihre	keine	**-e**
Dat.	den	ihnen	Ihren	keinen	**-n**

The sign of the nominative is **-r** or **-e** or no ending.
The sign of the accusative is **-n** for **der** words, **-e** for **die** words, no ending for **das** words.
The sign of the dative is **-m** for **der/das** words, **-r** for **die** words, **-n** for plural.

Can you see that the pattern of endings is the same for the words in one group? Learn the pattern, then you won't have to remember every single ending separately.

Verbs
Minimum endings to learn which will help you in most tenses.

ich	**-e**	**wir/sie/Sie**	**-en**
er/sie/es	**-t**		

Appendix

Strong verbs

Infinitive	*English*	*Present*	*Imperfect*	*Perfect*
bekommen	*to get*	bekommt	bekam	hat bekommen
bieten	*to offer*	bietet	bot	hat geboten
bitten	*to ask*	bittet	bat	hat gebeten
bleiben	*to stay*	bleibt	blieb	ist geblieben
brechen	*to break*	bricht	brach	hat gebrochen
empfehlen	*to recommend*	empfiehlt	empfahl	hat empfohlen
essen	*to eat*	ißt	aß	hat gegessen
fahren	*to drive*	fährt	fuhr	ist gefahren
fallen	*to fall*	fällt	fiel	ist gefallen
finden	*to find*	findet	fand	hat gefunden
fliegen	*to fly*	fliegt	flog	ist geflogen
geben	*to give*	gibt	gab	hat gegeben
gefallen	*to please*	gefällt	gefiel	hat gefallen
gewinnen	*to win*	gewinnt	gewann	hat gewonnen
halten	*to stop*	hält	hielt	hat gehalten
heißen	*to call*	heißt	hieß	hat geheißen
helfen	*to help*	hilft	half	hat geholfen
kommen	*to come*	kommt	kam	ist gekommen
lassen	*to let*	läßt	ließ	hat gelassen
laufen	*to run*	läuft	lief	ist gelaufen
leihen	*to lend*	leiht	lieh	hat geliehen
lesen	*to read*	liest	las	hat gelesen
liegen	*to lie*	liegt	lag	hat gelegen

Infinitive	*English*	*Present*	*Imperfect*	*Perfect*
nehmen	*to take*	nimmt	nahm	hat genommen
riechen	*to smell*	riecht	roch	hat gerochen
rufen	*to call*	ruft	rief	hat gerufen
scheinen	*to shine*	scheint	schien	hat geschienen
schlafen	*to sleep*	schläft	schlief	hat geschlafen
schneiden	*to cut*	schneidet	schnitt	hat geschnitten
schreiben	*to write*	schreibt	schrieb	hat geschrieben
schwimmen	*to swim*	schwimmt	schwamm	ist geschwommen
sehen	*to see*	sieht	sah	hat gesehen
singen	*to sing*	singt	sang	hat gesungen
sitzen	*to sit*	sitzt	saß	hat gesessen
sprechen	*to speak*	spricht	sprach	hat gesprochen
stehlen	*to steal*	stiehlt	stahl	hat gestohlen
steigen	*to climb*	steigt	stieg	ist gestiegen
sterben	*to die*	stirbt	starb	ist gestorben
tragen	*to carry*	trägt	trug	hat getragen
treffen	*to meet*	trifft	traf	hat getroffen
trinken	*to drink*	trinkt	trank	hat getrunken
vergessen	*to forget*	vergißt	vergaß	hat vergessen
vergleichen	*to compare*	vergleicht	verglich	hat verglichen
verlieren	*to lose*	verliert	verlor	hat verloren
waschen	*to wash*	wäscht	wusch	hat gewaschen
werfen	*to throw*	wirft	warf	hat geworfen
ziehen	*to pull*	zieht	zog	hat gezogen

Special verbs – *sein, haben, werden*

Sein (to be)

In all languages the verb 'to be' is different from the rest. **Sein** has irregular forms:

Present tense	**ich bin**	**wir sind**
	du bist	**ihr seid**
	er ist	**sie sind**
Imperative	**sei (du)**	**seid (ihr)**
	seien Sie	
Imperfect	**ich war**	**wir waren**
Perfect	**ich bin gewesen**	
Pluperfect	**ich war gewesen**	
Subjunctive	**ich wäre**	**wir wären**

Haben (to have)

Haben is more regular than **sein**:

Present tense	**ich habe**	**wir haben**
	du hast	**ihr habt**
	er hat	**sie haben**
Imperative	**hab (du)**	**habt (ihr)**
	haben Sie	
Imperfect	**ich hatte**	**wir hatten**
Perfect	**ich habe gehabt**	
Pluperfect	**ich hatte gehabt**	
Subjunctive	**ich hätte**	**wir hätten**

Werden

Present tense	**ich werde**	**wir werden**
	du wirst	**ihr werdet**
	er wird	**sie werden**
Imperfect	**ich wurde**	**wir wurden**
Perfect	**ich bin geworden**	
Pluperfect	**ich war geworden**	
Subjunctive	**ich würde**	**wir würden**

Werden has four very different uses.
1. = to become, followed by a noun or adjective.

2. to form the passive (see p.47).
Werden here has no meaning of its own. Its function is purely to help form the passive. Notice that there are no Umlauts.

3. to form the future tense (see p.25).
Again, **werden** is purely an auxiliary verb, helping another verb to form the future tense.

4. = would (see p.45).
Use **würde/würden** + the infinitive of the second verb, which goes to the end of the sentence.

Glossary of grammar terms

ACCUSATIVE describes the role that a noun or pronoun is playing in a particular sentence. Nouns and pronouns are in the accusative case if they are on the receiving end of the verb (=direct object) and also after certain other words and expressions. (See p.84.)

ADJECTIVE An adjective describes a noun. Words like 'pretty', 'big', 'thick', 'thin', 'easy' etc. are adjectives. (See p.110.)

ADVERB An adverb is a word which describes a verb or action. 'Slowly', 'well', 'beautifully', 'often'. 'sometimes' etc. are adverbs. (See p.119.)

AUXILIARY VERBS These are verbs which help other verbs to form a particular tense. For example, you use **haben** to help form the perfect tense (see p.18) and **werden** to help form the passive. (See p.47.)

CLAUSE A clause is a section of a sentence which contains a verb. If it can stand on its own, it is called a main clause. If it can not stand on its own, it is called a subordinate clause.

'I went to bed'	is a main clause.
'When I went to bed'	is a subordinate clause.

CONJUNCTION This is a word like 'and', 'but', 'so' etc. which joins two parts of a sentence together. (See p.73.)

DATIVE describes the role of a noun or pronoun in a particular sentence. The dative is used when you want to say 'to/from a person' (=indirect object) and also after certain words and expressions. (See p.88.)

DEFINITE ARTICLE = 'the'. (See p.94.)

DIRECT OBJECT A noun or pronoun is the direct object of a verb if it is on the receiving end of the action. Normally, the direct object comes after the verb in English, e.g. 'I ate an apple' – *an apple* is the direct object.

FUTURE TENSE describes actions which have not yet taken place. (See p.25.)

GENITIVE = possessive. You use the genitive case to translate English apostrophe 's or 'of'. (See p.92.)

IMPERATIVE = commands, orders. (See p.42.)

IMPERFECT TENSE is used for descriptive passages and incomplete action in the past. (See p.17.)

INDEFINITE ARTICLE = 'a/an'. (See p.97.)

INDIRECT OBJECT A noun or pronoun is an indirect object when it is not directly on the receiving end of the verb, e.g. 'I gave *her* a bunch of flowers' – *her* = *to her* and is an indirect object. (See p.88.)

INFINITIVE is the reference form of the verb you find in word lists and dictionaries. The English infinitive always has 'to' in front of it – 'to do', 'to see' etc.

NOMINATIVE A noun or pronoun is nominative if it is the subject of the verb, i.e. if it is doing the action. (See p.81.)

NOUN Words for objects, people, places are nouns. 'Pen', 'book', 'man', 'church', 'Berlin' etc. are all nouns. (See p.75.)

OBJECT See DIRECT OBJECT and INDIRECT OBJECT.

PASSIVE This is a special form of the verb which concentrates on the action being done, rather than on the person doing the action, e.g. 'He *has been injured*'; 'The ball *was lost*.' (See p.47.)

PAST PARTICIPLE In English, this is the '-ed' or '-en' form of the verb, e.g. 'talked', 'eaten', 'drunk' etc. (See p.19.)

PERFECT TENSE This form of the verb describes an action which happened in the past. (See p.18.)

PERSON = 'I, 'you', 'he', 'she', 'it'. (See p.13.)

PLUPERFECT TENSE This form of the verb describes action which happened a stage further back in the past than the perfect or imperfect tense. (See p.24.)

POSSESSIVE ADJECTIVE = 'my', 'your', 'his', 'her' etc. (See p.120.)

PREPOSITIONS are words like 'to', 'for', 'with' etc. (See p.126.)

PRONOUN e.g. 'I', 'you', 'he', 'she', 'it' etc. A pronoun is a word which refers to a person or thing. It is often used in place of a noun. (See p.99.)

SUBJECT A noun or pronoun is the subject of the verb when it is initiating the action, e.g. '*He* played football' – *He* is the subject of the verb 'played'. In English, the subject usually comes before the verb. (See p.81.)

SUBJUNCTIVE This is a special form of the verb which is used to describe actions which are in some way tentative, unreal, uncertain. The English words 'would', 'could' are usually reliable indicators for using the subjunctive. (See p.44.)

SUBORDINATE CLAUSE See CLAUSE.

TENSE Tense is the form of the verb which indicates *when* the action took/takes/will take place. (See p.13.)

VERB Words like 'eat', 'do', 'sit', 'stay' etc. which describe actions, states, position etc. are verbs. The verb is the focal point of every sentence. (See p.12.)

Index